RETIRING AS A CAREER

RETIRING AS A CAREER

Making the Most of Your Retirement

Betsy Kyte Newman

PRAEGER

Westport, Connecticut
London

Library of Congress Cataloging-in-Publication Data

Newman, Betsy Kyte, 1941–
    Retiring as a career : making the most of your retirement / Betsy Kyte Newman.
        p. cm.
    Includes bibliographical references and index.
    ISBN 0–275–98168–1 (alk. paper)
        1. Retirement—Planning—United States.   2. Retirement—United States—
Psychological aspects.   I. Title.
    HQ1064.U5N34 2003
    646.7'9'0973—dc21   2003053025

British Library Cataloguing in Publication Data is available.

Library of Congress Catalog Card Number: 2003053025
ISBN: 0–275–98168–1

First published in 2003

Praeger Publishers, 88 Post Road West, Westport, CT 06881
An imprint of Greenwood Publishing Group, Inc.
www.praeger.com

Printed in the United States of America

The paper used in this book complies with the
Permanent Paper Standard issued by the National
Information Standards Organization (Z39.48–1984).

10 9 8 7 6 5 4 3 2 1

Copyright Acknowledgments

The author and publisher gratefully acknowledge permission to reprint the following:

Reprinted from Joel S. Savishinsky: *Breaking the Watch: The Meanings of Retirement in America*. Copyright © 2000 by Joel S. Savishinsky. Used by permission of the publisher, Cornell University Press.

From *Taking Retirement* by Carl H. Klaus. Copyright © 1999 by Carl H. Klaus. Reprinted by permission of Beacon Press, Boston and Elizabeth Kaplan Library Agency.

Excerpts reprinted from Richard P. Johnson, *Creating a Successful Retirement*, Liguori Publications, 1999. A Redemptorist publication can be reprinted with permission of Liguori Publications, Liguori, MO 63057-9999. No other reproduction of this material is permitted.

From *The Spirit of Retirement* by James A. Autry, copyright © 2002 by James A. Autry. Used by permission of Prima Publishing, a division of Random House, Inc.

Excerpts © 2001 *Facts about Retiring in the United States* by Steven S. Shagrin, The H.W. Wilson Company. 950 University Avenue, Bronx, NY 10452-4297, www.hwwilson.com. Reprinted by permission of the publisher.

Extracts from *Fantasy Energizes Daily Life: The Magical Power to Aspire*, a lecture by Linda Weltner at the Harvard Divinity School in 2001. Used with permission of Linda Weltner.

To all my friends who helped in the creation of this "circular letter," please find herein your own message of love and profound gratitude from me.

Every book is in an intimate sense, a circular letter to the friends of him who writes it. They alone take his meaning; they find private messages, assurances of love and expressions of gratitude dropped at every corner. The public is but a generous patron.

—Robert Louis Stevenson, *Travels with a Donkey*

Contents

Acknowledgments

This book would never have happened without help from the following, to whom I am very grateful:

- To John Tew, M.D. and to Susan Hickenlooper who first (separately) suggested the project.

- To Susan Hickenlooper, Dr. Ann Wood Schlesinger, Dr. Judith Van Ginkel, and Tom White for critical reading and very astute feedback—and for helping me to develop my ideas.

- To Cathy and Tom Huenefeld for continuing interest, suggestions—and inspiration.

- To Elizabeth Lyon for her usual insightful editing and shrewd advice.

- To Mary Ellen and Bill Otto for invaluable suggestions and constant encouragement.

- To Johanna Orndorff, my assistant, for marvelous organization, unending interest, great suggestions, and for keeping the whole project on track.

- To all my terrific survey respondents, who shall remain anonymous, and who literally made this book possible. Thanks for your honesty and collective wisdom.

- And, once again, to George. If we ever retire, I look forward to spending it with you!

So You Want to Retire: Introduction to Why You Need This Book

The fact that you picked up this book indicates that you are interested in retirement. Perhaps either you or a loved one have recently retired or plan to retire soon. You may be experiencing a pinprick of anxiety as you face retirement, and you are wondering what you need to know to retire successfully. Or, perhaps you feel that all you need to know about retirement is financial planning—meeting your future economic needs by strategizing with a financial planner.

Of course, financial planning is an important part of retirement, although perhaps most Americans exaggerate its importance and rely on financial planning as their *only* preretirement strategy. Please note, however, that this book is primarily addressed to people who have already engaged in sound financial planning. This is a prerequisite for *any* contemplated retirement.

However, a calculator is not your best or only tool when you set out to create a successful retirement for yourself. While you need to be resourceful in planning your economic future in retirement, you need to be equally careful in accounting for your other "selves"—mental, spiritual, and emotional.

This is where *Retiring as a Career: Making the Most of Your Retirement* comes in. My goal is to help you plan your course, navigate the waters of retirement, and successfully reach your safe harbor. The focus of this book is not on finances, but rather on those things that create true satisfaction in retirement: health, friendships, relationships, spirituality, and full, satisfying range of activities.

Why this focus? Simply because many available retirement books have more than adequately covered finances and the necessity of financial planning. What seems underplayed, however, is an examination of all the other factors needed to create a successful retirement.

A quick word on the methodology of this book. While I have relied on current research on retirees and their needs, I also conducted a highly selective survey of actual retirees in 2002, focusing on the important issues of their own retirements. I surveyed more than 50 retirees, and while they do not constitute a true random sample, their backgrounds and experiences are diverse enough to reveal some interesting and useful information. The respondents were both male and female and included doctors, lawyers, other professionals, business owners, managers, teachers, bankers, and religious professionals, as well as single, divorced, and married people. At the time of my survey, these people had been retired from 6 months to 10 years and they ranged in age from 55 to 73, with a median age of 62. All were middle class or above, educated at least beyond the high school level, and lived on the East Coast, in the Midwest, or in the South.

Their most important qualifying characteristics were success and happiness in retirement and a willingness to share insights with those in the planning stages. (Although I realize there are many unhappy retirees, I thought I could learn more from the satisfied ones and those who had learned from their mistakes.)

All the respondents were asked the following questions:

1. What does "retirement" mean to you?
2. What precipitated your decision to retire? Was it by choice?
3. What was your picture of retirement at 25? Now? Are there any differences?
4. Do you know anyone whose retirement you admire? Who is your role model doing the kinds of things you like to do?
5. How much preplanning for your retirement did you do?
6. What resources, if any, did you use?
7. How do you (or will you) structure your retirement?
8. If you have already retired, how did you do in the first year? Is there any difference now?
9. Is your spouse retired?
10. How will you know if you have been successful in your own retirement (by your own definition)?
11. How does retirement affect your marriage? Your friends? Your other relationships?

12. In America we are often defined by what we do. Did your self-image change when you retired? Will (or did) your plan for retirement meet your need for self-worth and how?

13. Any other comments or suggestions?

Since 1900, Americans have been retiring less because of ill health or unemployment than in response to new economic conditions and leisure opportunities. Today, for the first time in our history, retirement is often more attractive than continuing to work. Americans now seem to view retirement as a norm, an expectation, even a right. Basic trends in retirement suggest that incomes drop but still remain adequate; that physical and mental health do not deteriorate when work stops; that although the content of activity changes, the level does not; that marital satisfaction generally tends to be high; that people tend to retire in place; and that (contrary to earlier views) people do not experience this life change as a major crisis.[1]

And yet these generalities about retirement remain broad, not individualized. Each person who retires must define retirement for himself or herself. In seeking out the respondents to my survey (through referrals, colleagues, and friends), I was eager to hear from these vital and interesting retirees just what they had done (or not done) to make their retirement successful. What most of them agreed on was the need to take specific steps to secure a healthy, active, friend-filled, and interesting retirement. Financial planning was only part (and for many *not* the most significant part) of their preretirement planning.

Typically, the retirees in my survey pondered significant, even cosmic questions, like the following:

• Was the life I've lived the one I wanted to live?
• What can I afford to do with it now?
• Did I fulfill my potential?
• Can I still be the person I once wanted to be?
• Who am I now, really?
• What kind of relationships do I want and need?

The remainder of this book will address the other necessary parts of retirement planning:

• Redefinition of retirement
• What to expect in retirement

- Avoiding common retirement pitfalls and maintaining self-esteem
- Special challenges for couples and women in retirement
- Structuring your time
- "Flunking" retirement and recovering from mistakes
- Finding meaning and purpose in your life through retirement

Along the way, you have the benefit of the insights and advice of the successful retirees in my survey. And because I remain a teacher at heart, at the end of each chapter I include summary points you may wish to remember!

A final word about the unusual title of this book, *Retiring As a Career: Making the Most of Your Retirement*. It reflects my growing understanding of retirement as a career in itself, deserving of and rewarding significant time and attention. Those who take on retirement energetically and thoughtfully seem to reap the best rewards. In fact, as you will discover during the course of reading this book, viewing your retirement as a career in itself encourages you to take it seriously, prepare for it well, and enjoy it as a meaningful and purposeful stage of life with intrinsic value.

But enough introduction. To get to the heart of creating a successful retirement career for yourself—read on!

NOTE

1. Joel S. Savishinsky, *Breaking the Watch*, 18 (includes a summary of major trends in retirement).

1

The American Dream?: Redefining Retirement for Yourself

The baby boom transforms each institution through which it passes. The pig is now devouring the python.

—John Naisbitt, *Megatrends*

A cherished part of the American dream is the idea of retirement—the pot of gold at the end of the worker's rainbow. Since the advent of Social Security in 1935, with its promise of financial security, the notion of the "golden years" crowned with leisure and unstructured time, has been the hallmark of the American myth of the good life.

Today's adults, who have no memory of the Great Depression, have a different view of retirement and are busily redefining it for themselves.

Before the mid-twentieth century, many people did not live long enough to retire. In medieval Europe, for example, war, starvation, and disease took care of the problem of aging. In some early Eskimo, American Indian, and Central African societies, the nonproductive elderly were cast off and left to die alone. In some parts of eighteenth-century India, the father in late middle age began freeing himself from materialistic concerns in order to turn over his home to his sons and become a wanderer in his old age.[1]

In 1882, English novelist Anthony Trollope examined the problem of when a person might be considered past his prime. In his novel *The Fixed Period,* he created Britannula, an imaginary island off the coast of New Zealand, and populated it with British colonists who set up their own Parliament.[2] This Parliament proposed the establishment of a "College of the Fixed Period," which all citizens would enter when they

In the past retirement was rarely a problem.

Old Solutions to Retirement, by George C. Lynch. *Source:* Eben Alexander Jr., M.D., "The 'Retired' Chairman Syndrome: A Twentieth Century Disease," *The Pharos*, (summer, 1984): 16–19. Reprinted with permission.

reached a certain age. At this certain age, citizens would be subjected to euthanasia so that they would be spared the horrors of poverty, disease, and infirmity. Of course, everyone argued over the exact age of the Fixed Period, and Parliament suggested a grandfather clause to exempt all old people currently living on the island. When they eventually decided on the age of 68, all 67-year-olds immediately began arguing that their birth records had the wrong date. To prevent future confusion, it was suggested that all newborns have their birth dates tattooed on their buttocks. Trollope ended the drama by having Britain send a gunboat to Britannula to establish its own rule.

Or I could also mention the Michael York movie, *Logan's Run* (1976), in which people were euthanized at age 30. No retirement problems there!

As we can see, the notion of a productive retirement—or even retirement itself—is a relatively new phenomenon.

Today's retirees are unique in human history. They are healthier, wealthier, better educated, and more skilled than old people were even

50 years ago. They possess vitality, energy, desire, direction, and remarkable insight. One of the challenges of our society is to take advantage of the wisdom and skills of retirees.

It is always useful to define the terms we use. What does the word "retirement" actually mean? In popular usage, it refers to the act of giving up a longtime job, career, or profession, usually due to increasing age. But, as Carl Klaus reminds us,[3] the word is derived from the French verb *retirer* (to draw again, pull back, to withdraw). In its basic sense, then, retirement suggests withdrawal to a secluded place, such as going to bed, or giving up ground, as in withdrawing from a battlefield. In other words, retirement is connected to the action of giving up, giving in, withdrawing from life itself. No wonder the notion of retirement has unpleasant connotations to many of us. Are we headed for passivity and defeat?

Perhaps we need to look further for a more positive definition of retirement. In contrast to the French word, the Spanish word for retirement is *jubilación*, which means not only "retirement" but also "pension,"[4] hence, the notion of celebration. This fascinating word study reminds us of how closely retirement is joined in our minds with financial security and stability. As my friend, Cathy, mischievously reminds me, "re-tirement time" suggests a time to "pump up" the tires of life, replacing a flat tire with something brand new. Today's retirees are people who are "re-tired," inflated, and ready for action. They have exchanged their old wheels for a new set and they're on a roll.

What do we want in retirement? Withdrawal or celebration? Or perhaps some combination of these ideas? Current retirees I interviewed offer different perspectives on retirement. They told me that retirement means:

"Leaving a job . . . that you have to do so you can pursue the things you'd like to do and not have to support yourself doing them."

"Not having to work and being able to do whatever and whenever I please."

"Every day is Saturday."

"Having the *time* to do what I want."

"An outdated word implying 'waiting for death!'"

"I am still doing a full-time job, but I consider myself retired. The distinction for me is the lack of a driving career objective. I work now because I want to and I feel completely free to stop when I don't want to work!"

"Leaving my job and living on savings rather than earnings."

"For me, retirement has meant being no longer committed to going to work every single day where there are constant expectations and requirements. It also meant no longer getting a paycheck, a retirement plan, and health care coverage. Retirement was a withdrawal from these arrangements."

"Gaining your freedom."

And, perhaps most tellingly,

"An opportunity to become one's SELF."[5]

What becomes obvious is that people's notions of retirement and their very personal definitions of it have changed over the years. When I asked my respondents for their pictures of retirement at age 25, their replies were significantly different:

"At 25, I never considered it!"

"At 25, I thought I should work until death. . . . [Now I know that] life is good but short."

"I never gave a thought to retirement in my youth. . . . Retirement was for people who were too old to be of value."

"It's for 'old' people. But now I see it as for people who've planned ahead so they have options and for people with new things to do."

"'Old and decrepit' versus 'leisure and active.'"

"An old person who is physically inactive and mentally slower."

"At 25, I think I was rigid. Now I am much more flexible and creative."

Younger people do not have an accurate notion of retirement. Several respondents, for example, reported increasing health concerns:

"At 25, I thought of retirement as fun and games. Now, health concerns are a new factor."

"My picture of retirement at age 25 was as it is now, but I never gave a thought to the fact that I might not be healthy. . . . I am now a Type II diabetic and am battling lymphoma."

"Thought I would be older when I retired and I thought I'd be with my (late) husband."

A large part of our definition of retirement is colored by the how we make the decision to retire. Did we retire by choice? Whose choice was our retirement? Some of my respondents who made their own decision to retire gave the following reasons.

"Work was no longer providing the satisfaction and stimulation to keep me motivated."

"It was planned for years and motivated by the desire for change. I wanted to keep growing and learning."

"I wanted to do other things."

"All the endless responsibilities and the inflexible schedule meant that the best of me was spent outside my home and apart from my family. . . . This became more evident as I got older."

"Had been planning for early retirement, but a pending change in retirement eligibility made me decide to retire now."

"Both parents died in their early seventies, and there are so many things I want to do."

"There were three principal factors in my decision to retire. First, I saw too many people working too long and not having the time to pursue other interests. (I had two friends who retired at 70 and died a year later.) Second, I had a situation in the business in which I was a principal owner that was not to my liking and I found myself unable to turn that situation around. Finally, there was enough value in the company, that I could sell my ownership and realize significant proceeds from my stock sale."

"An intense desire to experience other sides of myself by doing different things. The choice was mine."

For some, by contrast, retirement was not chosen, but forced upon them (either directly or indirectly) with bittersweet consequences:

"I retired by choice, but because my options became unattractive to me."

"At some point in almost everyone's career, the pyramid narrows and there is nowhere to go. . . . For most of us, that means stepping aside into a staff role."

As one woman tellingly remarked, "It's like a divorce; it's good only if it was your idea in the first place."

Some retirees created their own model of retirement, often after several false starts. Bob, a retired executive in his late fifties, confesses that:

My first year was terrible, I tried to play more sports but I don't like to play golf every day. . . . Then I volunteered for several things but did not find any of them satisfactory.

For one retired 62-year-old architect, on the other hand, the first-year experience was more satisfying:

The first year was wonderful. . . . I never realized how much stress I was operating under in my business life until it was no longer there.

For another, her first year of leisure was idyllic:

The first year I took a complete sabbatical, I took courses, relaxed, and enjoyed life. Since then, I now read more, volunteer three days a week. I'm freer, more interested in sports.

Clearly, there is no one-size-fits-all model of retirement. Rather, as we shall see, retirement is a highly individual process, viewed differently by each person and refined and redefined according to his or her temperament, expectations, and experience.

For some, retirement presents a prospect of unstructured time, free from agendas and schedules. But for others, retirement means changing one set of expectations and obligations for another, creating a self-chosen regime of activities, family time, community volunteer work, and recreation. For many, the first year of retirement is a trial-and-error process, involving many shifts in expectations and perspectives, and sometimes radical changes as one actually lives out the reality of retirement. After the first year of leisure, some choose to return to paid work, whereas others, equally devoted to feeling productive, choose to volunteer their time in worthwhile charitable efforts or in mentoring newcomers in their previous profession. For many, their true retirement begins after that first, often traumatic year, when it takes on its own unique blend of work (paid or unpaid) and creative leisure.

As one retired teacher in her sixties describes her time:

Structure is what I am trying to get away from. I don't want each day mapped out with a "must do" agenda. I want to be able to take advantage of all kinds of things that are available, often for a limited time. I look forward to planning a vacation that is not predicated on a school schedule. I don't want to feel guilty if I am not producing something meaningful all the time.

In addition to personal temperament, events also play a part in both the structure and vision of retirement. The recently retired teacher continues:

> This is my first year of retirement, and the biggest bump in the road has been the events of September 11, 2001. All the following months since then have been reminders that I need to stop and smell the roses, not to get caught up in the unimportant, and to slow down!

Unexpected events—illness, divorce, financial changes, family crises, caregiver responsibilities, and unplanned opportunities—can profoundly alter one's experience of retirement. Moreover, as we shall see in subsequent chapters, retirement is a time of life that can change all of our relationships. There are also gender differences. Men and women experience retirement differently. In general, men have more difficulty leaving behind their work and career identities, whereas women are more likely to feel financial and social vulnerability. (This, of course, may change as more women enter and leave the workforce.)

But even these generalities are challenged by many men and women who experience just the opposite. Like every other stage of life, retirement is a unique, individual process.

As our population ages, we have come to acknowledge retirement as a new, if uncharted, stage of life. Of course, men and women have always retired from work, but never before have so many done it so soon. Until the twentieth century, most people worked until they died. History shows us that in the eighteenth and nineteenth centuries, people with enough money—the landed gentry, for example, or rich merchants— would retire to the country, but most people just worked and worked till it killed them. We need to remember that the middle class is a comparatively modern invention.

Americans can now expect to spend up to one-third of their lives after they retire. For many of those years, according to Phyllis Moen, director of the Cornell Applied Gerontology Research Institute, they will be in good health. Moen also points out that by 2030 there will be more Americans over 65 than under 18. "Our research," Moen writes, "indicates that about half of retirees retire unexpectedly with little or no planning and that the retirement transition is extraordinarily diverse, not at all a routinized exit."[6]

Moen's groundbreaking study, the *Cornell Retirement and Well-Being Study*, provides valuable information to anyone studying today's varieties of retirement. As a random sampling of 762 men and women between ages 50 and 72, the study examines transition choices, decisions, and

productive involvement on the part of retirees. Moen notes that two
million Americans retire annually and that by 2010 the number will
swell to three million.[7] Her study further suggests that we must, as a
society, come to terms with this healthy and capable, yet typically ig-
nored, group of retirees in their fifties, sixties, seventies, and eighties.
Other key findings in Moen's study are striking:

> Although 93 percent of those between 65 and 72 are retired, one in four
> of the retired still work (15 percent of women and 35 percent of men),
> most part time.
>
> Women tend to retire later, have fewer financial resources, and view re-
> tirement as more problematic than men do.
>
> Volunteering and caregiving actively increase with age (45 percent
> volunteer).
>
> Most of the retirees Moen studied are enjoying retirement, and family is
> a key source of satisfaction.

Moen concludes that "the post-retirement years have been too often
cast as the post-productive years. With few family and job obligations,
individuals in this period of comparative 'rolelessness' can be especially
at risk of social isolation and the onset of poor health. . . . We need
more research on the links between productive activities and health and
ways to foster competence and productivity in this new life phase."[8]

Retirees are expected to live out their life spans in comfort. In television ads and magazine spreads, we are treated to the sight of happily
retired insurance and retirement-plan customers. These ads always fea-
ture a couple—handsome, relaxed, and young-looking—either walking
the beach or traveling to exotic locales. Those ads do, in fact, represent
some retirees.

But for a second category of retirees, the "golden years" may seem a
bit tarnished. Many are, sadly, no longer part of a couple and must spend
these years without their mates. Many are also without adequate funds,
isolated from their families, and have few contacts with former colleagues and friends.

There is, however, a third group, those who have adequate income
and close family and friends, but for whom retirement is a form of forced
inactivity and unhappiness. These retirees feel useless and somewhat
resentful, especially if they have been forced into retirement by age
restrictions at work.

Some of these retirees return to their old careers in different forms,
others seek out employment in new fields, and still others become vol-

unteers. Some start a new avocation after retirement. Others continue to feel useless.

In the following chapters, we will examine the changing nature of retirement. We will look at both the promises and the caveats, at the rewards and pitfalls of this challenging transition. Finally, we will suggest some pathways to success in this new stage of life.

Points to Remember

- Retirement is a very personal concept. Each person defines it individually.
- Because of this individuality, and because of the changing nature of retirement in a healthy, longer-living population, some thought about retirement before the actual event is important.
- In retirement, as in most clothing, one size does *not* fit all.
- Understanding and preparing for retirement increases the chance for success.

NOTES

1. Eben Alexander Jr., M.D., "The 'Retired' Chairman Syndrome," 16.
2. Anthony Trollope, *The Fixed Period.*
3. Carl H. Klaus, *Taking Retirement*, 11.
4. Ibid., 124.
5. These and all other anonymous quotations in the book are responses from my Retirement Questionnaire 2002.
6. Phyllis Moen, "Americans Retiring Earlier but Living Longer," *Successful Aging*, 2.
7. Ibid., 2.
8. Ibid., 2. (For reprints of this article, access www.news.cornell.edu/release/feb96/aaasmoen.ssl.html.)

2

⟨⟨⟨

What Do You Need to Know?:
Planning Ahead

Ever more people today have the means to live, but nothing to live for.
—Viktor Frankel

To be for one day entirely at leisure is to be for one day immortal.
—Chinese proverb

We all like to know what to expect of the next stage in life. Because
retirement looms as such a significant issue for us aging baby boomers,
we want answers to some urgent questions: What do we have to know
about retirement before we embark on it? Is planning helpful or is it a
waste of time? And what about the crucial decisions surrounding retirement, such as: Where will we live? Should we move? With whom will
we share our retirement? How will we shape this apparently endless
expanse of time we are now facing? This chapter will respond to some
of these issues, as we look to ways to approach retirement planning.

TO PLAN OR NOT TO PLAN?

When asked about planning, the retirees I surveyed gave interesting,
if somewhat contradictory, advice. Many of them saw planning for retirement as crucial. A retired physician in my survey made the following
comment.

My image of retirement has been refined by observation. I recognize that it is important to continue to live in a community where there is good medical care and where you and your family are close. More importantly, it is essential to be involved in an essential work. . . . I engaged in extensive preplanning. I worked on my next position (office change) for three years. I became intensely involved in business and charitable activities and wrote a second book. All were done in preparation for remaining in a vibrant community, continuing a meaningful work, and being mentored by friends and loved ones.

Clearly, this doctor planned for a retirement as active and productive as most people's working lives. Although not everyone would define his retirement as precisely and specifically as he did, a retired teacher of 60 echoed his sentiments on planning ahead:

I did a lot of planning in terms of when it would be right for me. I informed the appropriate people so my position could be filled and I carved out a small part-time job working on curriculum development. This has been more work than I expected but it has been a nice easing out of the scene. The other component to preplanning was my strong feeling that I not jump into countless volunteer jobs. I had done a great deal of this sort of work full time, and I was not and am not interested in simply filling my days with a lot of fragmented efforts simply to look active and busy. I intend to keep this low profile for a year. Then I will test the waters in areas where I can use my talents best without feeling I am just putting in my time to keep active.

One female personnel executive says she planned "fairly much, from seeking counsel of a financial analyst in the early 1990s to getting personal counseling to deal with my fears." She is one of the few savvy retirees who planned for emotional as well as financial needs.

However, it is only fair to point out that a significant minority of my survey (about 10 percent) insisted that a lot of planning ahead for retirement was not really necessary. One retired (and very successful) businessman said, for example, that he planned "very little" because "just like starting a business—the more you investigate and try to figure everything out, the less likely you are to do it."

A retired architect who owned his own business admits:

I didn't do a lot of preplanning for retirement; in fact, I was as surprised as anyone when I made the decision to sell my ownership in the business two years ago and retire. I had tracked my financial situation on a regular basis, particularly as the idea of retirement appeared on the horizon, and I came to the realization that there was enough value there to permit me to do without the income stream from my business. It was one of my more sudden life decisions.

A woman who owned a travel agency admits that she, too, did not plan ahead, but she "did go from full time–plus to part-time employment to ease the transition. That did clarify the decision to retire fully." In contrast, a physician and former hospital chief of staff currently in the process of retiring, says:

> I never planned my life, it just happened. I don't think you can plan your future life either. What I did do was attempt to create a retirement environment in my work life. This involved cutting back hours and no longer accepting reappointment or reelection to the various responsibilities that accrue as part of the full-time job. It was amazing how easy the job was without them; I felt retired working full time. Then it was simply a matter of showing up less often. You and your spouse have to make some big decisions, move or stay, etcetera; once those are made or deferred, you are on your way for another adventure. Hope it turns out as well as the last one.

Most retirees who planned for retirement concentrated on their future financial needs. Another physician said he planned "a fair amount— financial and arranging 'service' work." A recently retired female banker planned "one or two years ahead—made a major volunteer commitment and planned exercise routines." Another man declared, "Quite a bit of planning was required to decide on the location to retire and the amount of dollars that would be needed." A businesswoman's extensive planning related to "*where* to live, not *what* to do." Another retired banker (a male in his sixties) says he spent "many hours planning until I felt comfortable with financial arrangements." And then he adds, tellingly, "Years ago I developed a value-centered philosophy of life that I found comforting and fulfilling." Most of my other respondents met extensively with financial-planning professionals but did not plan much else. One retiree's preplanning simply centered around "enjoying life. I thought about all the books I would like to read, all the museums I would like to visit, the symphonies I would like to hear, etcetera."

PLANNING FOR EMOTIONAL AND SOCIAL NEEDS

An interesting new trend in retirement planning sets both emotional and financial needs as top priorities in charting the course for later life.

In January 2002, *Time* magazine[1] reported that "new style" retirees are learning from the mistakes of their predecessors, who merely followed the call of climate and amenities into an isolated paradise. Similarly, in a mid-1990s study of 1,500 retirees from a Fortune 500 company who settled in the southern United States, an overwhelming number of participants admitted that they had not planned well enough for their emotional needs or how they would spend their time.

In the *Time* article, Marlene Rosenkolter, a gerontologist and dean of the school of nursing at the Medical College of Georgia, identifies six areas in which planning for emotional fulfillment is critical to a happy retirement: roles, relationships, self-esteem, support groups, life structure, and use of time. She notes that friendship is a crucial ingredient in each of these six areas. The *Time* article goes on to describe a trend of "new style" retirees—tightly knit groups of friends who decide to retire and move together to a retirement community, where they can continue to socialize, interact, and support each other through widowhood, illness, and dependence.[2]

Clearly, the new style of these retirees reveals careful planning, and also an awareness of the emotional needs that previously may have been answered by work. Marc Freedman, author of *Prime Time*, a book about aging baby boomers, suggests that this new form of retirement—involving community planning—reflects research showing that what people miss most after retirement is the "sense of purpose, identity, and relationships that come with work." Freedman predicts that more retired people will look to second or third careers in order to satisfy social as well as financial needs.[3]

Since most of us work for the greater part of our lives, work provides us with benefits that we take for granted, often not realizing that these benefits have been elevated in our subconscious to the level of needs. These needs must continue to be satisfied or we will feel somehow lost or diminished. In *Creating a Successful Retirement*, Richard P. Johnson suggests that work provides us with five basic needs that contribute mightily to our overall sense of life satisfaction:

1. Financial remuneration
2. Time management
3. Sense of usefulness
4. Status
5. Socialization[4]

We cannot simply ignore these five needs without emotional, psychological, and spiritual consequences. Many of us know someone whose retirement was diminished, or even destroyed, by their failure to pay attention to these needs and either replace or satisfy them in retirement. Later chapters of this book will deal in greater detail with each of these five needs; for now, it is enough to note that some planning for social and emotional needs should be taken into account as we think ahead about retirement.

At this point, take some time to think about your own personal goals, and talk candidly with your spouse or companion about the following areas of your lives:

Finances

Physical health

Travel

Education

Vocation

Emotional health

Social needs

Spirituality

Home environment

These topics will form the basis of our discussions for the rest of this book.

RETIREMENT AS A PROCESS

Some current researchers on retirement suggest that we need to think of retirement as a gradual process rather than a singular event.[5] Joel S. Savishinsky, a gerontologist and social scientist at Ithaca College, describes retirement as an ongoing process during which we get used to being retired and coping with its demands, which include establishing a new identity, addressing our dreams and disappointments, developing a new sense of purpose, adjusting our relationships, and learning to look at our past and future with increasing self-awareness. He comments that while the statistical studies on retirement focus on the issues that researchers and politicians are interested in, these issues are not necessarily what retirees themselves care about. In accord with my own sampling, Savishinsky's larger survey reveals that retirees have typically pondered more cosmic and interesting questions like *who am I now* and *what is the purpose of my life now.*

RITUALS, RITES, SPACE, AND TIME

Symbols and rituals are part of all life transitions, and as such are a valuable part of the retirement experience. In any transition, there are three parts: an ending of what has gone on before, a neutral or in-between phase, and a new beginning.[6] Before we can begin a new phase, life after retirement, we have to let go of the old phase, the working life we have known up to now. Because we are human, we may need to mark these passages with concrete, physical expressions of the realities we are experiencing. Therefore, we need rituals, rites of passage, or cere-monies that mark the ending of one way of life before we can begin a new one.

The term "rites of passage" refers to the way that societies mark life's transitions. In Western societies, we have rituals for birth and death, puberty and marriage, election of new political or religious leaders, in-itiations into secret societies (e.g., fraternities or sororities), and even for entering new seasons (e.g., Memorial Day and Labor Day picnics and celebrations). These rituals mark rites of passage from one stage of life to another. While they are ceremonial and symbolic, they also help us to recognize that reality will be different for us after the ritual. Again, because we are *physical* creatures, we need *physical* symbols to make con-crete a non-physical reality.

A ritual is a repeatable set of actions designed to help us remember or reenact something important. Rituals help us to move from one stage of life to the next by transforming our identities and helping us to rec-ognize that something is truly ending, so that we can move on. In our culture, however, we tend to downplay ritual as "too corny" and to eliminate many celebrations. One of the most important tasks for the retiree is to recognize, acknowledge, and even to celebrate the fact that his or her work life (or at least this stage of it) has ended and it's time move on to something else. Rituals, whether they are formal or informal rites of passage, gatherings, or words of appreciation and farewell, are important to both the retiree and the coworkers who are soon to be left behind. Just as high school graduation marks the end of one phase of life before young adulthood can begin, so retirement celebrations give our minds and hearts the chance to recognize and embrace the new reality of retirement. Failure to mark this phase can have unintended consequences, as one of my survey respondents discovered:

I thought I didn't want—or need—all that retirement rigmarole and so I told them at work just to skip it and treat my last day like any other. I said goodbye briefly and went home. The next day, and all the days after I just went about my life, trying to get used to the idea of being retired. . . . It took me months to realize what was missing, why I felt vaguely dissatisfied. I felt a giant anticlimax, a "so what?" I never really felt like I retired. I just tried to carry on as usual and it didn't work. . . . If I were doing it all again, I'd have it all, the party, the jokes, the gifts and even the roast. I guess I needed that to make it seem real to me.

The traditional retirement ritual—including creating a guest list and the experiencing the party itself, with jokes, gifts, and humorous toasts—is how we mark this significant change in our life. We can look forward to our retirement ritual with anticipation or dread, and look back on it with fondness or sadness, but the ritual does offer a way to come to terms with reality. It's very hard to get on with your new life when you really have not said goodbye to your old one. As one of my survey respondents declared, "Retirement necessarily encompasses *change*." Marking that change makes it real to us down to our souls.

Rituals are not techniques for doing something, but rather lenses through which we magnify the experience of something we are living through. Rituals of passage are simply a way of focusing and making visible the natural pattern of dying and renewal that constantly operates throughout the universe.

In retiring, you are saying goodbye to the work that has been a major occupation of your waking life. Even if your working life hasn't been entirely happy, the giving up of it represents, at some level, a loss. You need to respond to that loss by at least acknowledging its reality in some concrete, physical way.

This transition, like all changes, involves death and rebirth. In a sense, your old self-as-worker has to die so that a new self-as-retiree can be born. You need rituals to help you respond to endings and losses. In the case of a retirement ritual, it helps to bid farewell to all that has gone before, to disengage from the past, and to disidentify with a former self that will be no more.

A useful analogy to the need for ritual, rite, and ceremony is to think of the familiar ritual of high school graduation. The reality of the transition is simply that you have finished your formal, legally required schooling and are now eligible to begin your post–high school life: college, job, army, or some other field of endeavor. And yet, the change signified by the transition is profound: it marks the end of childhood and the beginning of adulthood. You move into the responsibilities and privileges of an adult life. To mark this profound change, we surround the simple act of finishing the twelfth grade with ceremonies and rites: a diploma, the donning of a cap and gown, marching with classmates to the strains of "Pomp and Circumstance," and photographs, handshakes, awards, and parties; all these things make real to us the change that graduation represents. Before we move ahead into a new life, we look back to acknowledge, mourn, and celebrate the high school life that we are leaving. (If for some reason you had to miss your own high school graduation, you know the feeling of incompletion that resulted. There is a sense of loss, of failing to close the circle, which indicates how important life rituals are to us.)

Similarly, retirement is a kind of graduation from working life into what follows. Ignoring or skipping rituals associated with retirement robs the event of some of its significance and may lead to a sense of loss and incompleteness. People are not merely logical beings, they are full of feelings too. We are not just literal minded; we also react symbolically to events. We need symbols to mark the end of an old identity as well as those that reinforce a new identity.

What are some of the rituals we associate with retirement? Parties, testimonial dinners, cards, skits, gifts, and gold watches have become associated symbolically with retirement. They are symbols that help us mark the reality of a major life change. Like all symbols, they partake of the reality they represent. For example, parties, testimonials, and "roasts" celebrate (seriously or humorously) the contributions the individual has made to the workplace. The gifts are tokens of appreciation but also symbolize the reality of the new life to come: a gold watch (unstructured time), golf clubs (leisure and hobbies), tickets and reservations (time to travel). Gifts and parties help us to celebrate the past and accept the future of retirement. So rituals are a significant part of retirement as we shall see.

Creating Your Own Rituals

For those retirees whose company skipped the retirement ritual (or who perhaps chose voluntarily to forgo any celebrations on their behalf), don't feel that you can't make up for what you might have lost. If you're convinced by now that there is validity and vitality in the use of rituals in retirement, it's not too late to create your own rite! Here's how you might begin.

If you are in the preretirement stage, but know your company will not sponsor any special rituals, take some time now to plan what would be meaningful to you. Answer the following questions for yourself, and then use your answers as a blueprint for designing your own retirement ritual. (It helps to write out your answers in a notebook or journal.)

1. What are the things you have enjoyed most about working?
2. What are you proudest of in terms of your accomplishments at this workplace? In this particular job?
3. Name the people who have influenced and mentored you in your career and specify what you have learned from each one.
4. Which people will you miss the most when you retire? (Don't forget to include favorite clients or customers as well as coworkers.)
5. What did you enjoy about your work environment (i.e., locale, office, social interaction, commute, etc.)?
6. What will you NOT miss at work?
7. What have you learned through your work?
8. How have you grown personally as a result of this work?
9. Is there any symbolic personal memento you can take with you as you leave, to remind you of your accomplishments at work? (Perhaps a picture, plaque, desk item, or special chair that you could request?) Make sure you request this *ahead* of time!

After you have answered these questions and reflected on what work has meant to you, prepare a little private ceremony of farewell. This can be anywhere and time you like; merely plan it so that you allow yourself enough time to bid a proper farewell—not just to your workplace but to your job itself. (Some people like to do this at the end of the day when the office is empty.) Take some time to walk around the building and through all the office areas you've used, recalling all the positive things you've experienced there, and say a silent farewell. You may wish to perform some small action like discarding old notes or removing personal items to make the farewell more ceremonial and real. This is the time to take the personal memento you have requested, which will serve as a proud reminder of your work identity as you begin a new phase. Along with creating a work memento, you may wish to discard something (a name plate or uniform pin) that symbolizes your old work identity—both steps of retaining and discarding are important.

Take a mental journey around your old workplace and say a personal goodbye. If you are still in contact with former coworkers, you may want to let them know how much they have meant to you and how much you appreciate them now that you've retired.

A final word about rituals: they remain powerful even after retirement. Many retired people give structure and meaning to their days by creating and embracing their own self-designed ritual actions particular to their own retirement. For some, it is a daily visit to church; for others, their rituals might be an early morning walk on the beach, a convivial cup of coffee at a local restaurant, or an exercise class at the local gym. Rituals can comfort us, sustain us, and remind us symbolically of the new realities of this stage of life.

Travel

One of the more important rites of passage during retirement is travel. The simple movement from one place to another is symbolic of moving out of one stage of life into another. Many potential retirees see travel as a nice option, a frill, perhaps, but not a necessary part of retirement. However, travel is something to consider as a ritual, as it offers possibilities that may greatly enhance your retirement.

First of all, travel offers a concrete reminder of the reality of the retirement state. Planning a trip, however short, to follow immediately after your retirement is a useful way to bring home to yourself the fact that you have, in fact, retired! A simple change of scene and the act of packing up and moving to another location, however briefly, serves to indicate to yourself, as well as to anyone else, that you have entered into a new life stage. It allows you a neutral pause in order to gather your thoughts, to reflect on the great life transition you have just made and focus your attention on the next step. Free from the normal distractions of your everyday life, you can ponder your present and future in new and different surroundings.

Moreover, travel offers other benefits to the new retiree as well: learning, culture, new friends, activities, hobbies, fresh ways of being and interacting with people, the possibility of reinvention of self, and even spiritual insight. Of course, a simple weekend jaunt won't offer all of these potential benefits, but they do accompany the notion of travel itself.

One of the most exciting and attractive aspects of travel is the opportunities that it offers for learning—about geography, language, art, culture, business—and about oneself. The mere fact of moving from one geographic spot to another opens up new horizons and makes possible the discovery of new people and new ideas. It's not only foreign or exotic travel that offers such possibilities; even a short road trip within the region or a lengthy tour of the United States rewards the curious and motivated tourist. As one of my respondents described:

> The trip my wife and I took in our van across the United States really opened my eyes. I had no idea of the separate regional cultures flourishing across this country . . . and the many fascinating local histories that we unearthed. . . . We started out with a rather vague desire to drive West and once we got started, discovered a wealth of attractions from battle-fields to quaint and unusual museums. It was one of the best trips I ever took.

And of course, everything that can be said about exploring new local cultures and learning about American history is even more true of foreign travel. So many people have postponed extensive travel for most of their working lives that retirement is the first time they have time and money to indulge in it. And what a revelation overseas travel can be! You can pursue a specific cultural interest (art or archeology), master a foreign language, or attend a formal study program in a foreign country to expand your cultural horizons. Chapter 8 will expand on options for learning while traveling; it's enough to note here that learning opportunities offer one of the most significant benefits of travel to retirees.

Along with the excitement of discovering interesting cultures, travel offers the chance to make interesting new friends. Possibly because you are in a novel environment and removed from some of the normal restraints and inhibitions of home, many people find it easier to break the ice while traveling and to introduce themselves to fellow travelers and local citizens they meet along the way. Rewarding, lifelong friendships can arise from a memorable trip.

In addition, travel can yield new activities and hobbies for the retiree, particularly adventure or exotic travel. Many a former couch potato has discovered the joys of white-water rafting, downhill skiing, or mountain climbing as a result of being part of an adventure trip. The truly adventurous sign up for a trip on their own, without the comfort and safety of a friend or spouse. As one retired widow, Mary, discovered:

> My safari to Africa opened my eyes—and my life—in many ways. Not only did I make terrific new friends (I took the trip on my own) but I discovered a brand new and unsuspected passion—wild animals. When I returned home, I decided to become active as a volunteer at my local zoo. Now I am a docent and volunteer in the public relations office. I love

it—it's given me a new lease on life. And all because I had the courage to take that trip!

That brings us to another, more subtle benefit of travel: a new personality style. For many people, being away from home and from their normal friends (and the friends' perceptions of them) gives them permission to change and expand their ways of being and interacting with people. For the first time, they may overcome shyness and inhibition and allow a new personality to develop and blossom. In a sense, they give themselves permission to reinvent themselves in the safe environment of a whole new geographical location.

And finally, one can use travel as a vehicle for a spiritual journey, as an occasion for spiritual insight. For those who travel alone, they may have the chance to discover strengths they didn't have, and to learn who they are as an individual by venturing out alone to a new place. Traveling and studying new cultures and involving oneself with so many new people strengthens one—and reveals strengths and confidence never before suspected.

And for couples, the use of travel as a spiritual journey of awakening can be equally profound. James Autry, in his book on retirement, describes the benefit of the spiritual journey shared by a recently retired couple, Gene and Pat:

> Once my husband and I touched the richness of exploration, it became part of us and allowed us to see beyond appearances to embrace a larger possibility. . . . Our choices for travel took us to natural places like the Amazon, Galapagos Islands, Tahiti on a Barefoot Windjammer Cruise. Never did we seek out a big hotel on the beach. . . . We hiked through volcanoes and to the top of mountains, into botanical gardens and waterfalls. Yosemite became our favorite place to celebrate our wedding anniversary, and on our thirty-second and thirty-fourth, we hiked to the top of Yosemite Falls.[7]

Autry describes another retired couple, John and Holly, whose focus on spiritual insight is part of the lure of travel for them. Their travel planning and the journey itself focus on the attitudes and intentions they bring to the trip and not just the trip alone. Before planning a trip, they begin by reading everything they can discover about the areas they want to visit. Instead of focusing just on tourist guides, they delve into history, commentary, and novels about the place that interests them. "We try to put more meaning into travel than just seeing sights," says John. Adds his wife, Holly, "They are not shopping trips, they are experience trips. And we never took a trip that was not just wonderful, even a simple drive along the Mississippi River."[8]

What exactly are they trying to learn or discover? Again, John answers:

> We try to get out of the big cities into the countryside. . . . We like to make opportunities to be with local people, to try to experience them in some small way. . . . We want to travel with fresh eyes, we want to experience a place and its people and not just observe them. We realize there are many different cultural approaches to life and that ours is not necessarily right or wrong. We're interested in how we approach our lives versus what it would be like if we'd been born in the place we're visiting. We look for the chance to try on different backgrounds for a while.[9]

Both Savishinsky and Klaus stress the importance of marking a travel-transition to a new life as part of the process of retirement. Since one of the most important developments in our past century has been the "invention" of retirement as a new stage of life, complete with its own name, organizations, magazines, and economic and legal infrastructures, plus full-blown planned communities, it follows that retirement should have its own ceremonies, symbols, and rituals.[10]

Travel often marks a separation between the periods of a life. The journey may be long or short, but it allows new retirees to separate from work, hometown, and the former daily round of life and social ties. Going somewhere else allows retirees to reflect on the past and think about what they want in their future. As the novelist Lawrence Durrell observed, "Journeys . . . flower spontaneously out of the demands of our natures—and the best of them not only lead us outwards in space but inwards as well. Travel can be one of the most rewarding forms of introspection."[11] Several of my survey respondents mentioned that when they returned from their postretirement trip (however short it was), their new identity as a retiree was "more real" to them. As one woman said, "After my trip, except for the absence of work, things around me were the same, yet I felt somehow changed. It was easier to go away and come back as a different person than to simply change in place."

Retirement Space and Time

In addition to rituals and travel in retirement, enough time and sufficient space also seem to be important. In retirement, which marks a significant *time* change, people also need to know where in *space* they belong—where they are coming from, where they are going to, and where they will henceforth fit in. Just as the rituals (ceremony, party, gifts, trip) help them to negotiate when and how to retire, and their stance on planning (or not planning) helps them to frame what retirement might involve, they also have to grapple with the questions of *where* their retirement will be lived out, and what places, people, and things they will surround themselves with. (We will deal with this more fully in chapter 11, when we further revisit the importance of ritual, place, and travel for the retiree.)

As noted above, the decision to move or not to move is crucial, and the related task of sorting through one's material world is likewise critical to one's sense of identity and to moving on to the next stage of life. My survey revealed that home, land, community, and possessions carry different weights and meanings for people. A retired businessman, for example, relished the chance to change:

> I really like the idea of scaling down, starting over and reinventing myself in retirement. Part of that involved getting rid of a lot of "stuff" and moving to a smaller, more manageable home in a new city.

But a retired teacher found the opposite to be true: "I wanted to stay in familiar surroundings and grow old with my own friends and lifelong treasures."

As we consider the choices of where to live and whom to live with in retirement, we are forced to struggle with some of the basic, though often contradictory, themes in our culture. These include the tensions between freedom and rootedness, adventure and security, family responsibility and personal fulfillment. Here again, one size does *not* fit all. One flavor, or one type and location of residence, does not fit everyone. Since retirement is played out and explored in our own life *time* and life *space*, as we plan our retirement and decide where to make our lives, it is wise to heed the ancient Greek advice to "know thyself." Retirement is indeed the gift of time, but this gift carries a burden, which is the rediscovery of choice. With retirement comes the responsibility of making up our own new life.

Points to Remember

- Planning should address our emotional and social needs as well as our financial requirements.
- It is important to recognize the five basic needs (finance, time man-

agement, purpose, status, and socialization) fulfilled by work and to plan for their replacements.

- Retirement is a chance to reinvent ourselves, to choose where and how we will live for the rest of our lives.

- The more we know about ourselves and our needs, the better we can prepare for retirement.

NOTES

1. Francine Russo, "Buddy System," *Time* Magazine, 20 January 2002, G1–G3.

2. Ibid.

3. Marc Freedman, *Prime Time*.

4. Richard P. Johnson, *Creating a Successful Retirement*.

5. See especially Joel S. Savishinsky, *Breaking The Watch*; and Carl H. Klaus, *Taking Retirement*.

6. For a full explanation of the phases of transition, see William Bridges's *Transitions*.

7. James A. Autry, *The Spirit of Retirement*, 39.

8. Ibid., 229.

9. Ibid., 230.

10. Joel S. Savishinsky, *Breaking the Watch*, 244–45; and Carl H. Klaus, *Taking Retirement*, 17.

11. Lawrence Durrell, *Bitter Lemons*, 1.

3

⬥⬥⬥

What Happens Next?: What to Expect in Retirement

> Americans hardly ever retire from business: they are either carried
> out feet first or they jump from the window.
> —A. L. Goodhart, American lawyer

Spoken at the beginning of the twentieth century, A. L. Goodhart's
words give us an idea of just how differently we see retirement today, a
hundred years later. The demographics of retirement are unmistakable.
Today, more people are retiring every day, and the numbers are continuing to grow.

Moreover, since the early twentieth century Americans have been
retiring less because of illness or unemployment (the old standard reasons for retiring) than in response to what one of my survey respondents
called "new economic and cultural opportunities." Because retirees are
in better health and are living longer than before, they see retirement
as an attractive option. This pattern persists even in the face of such
recent labor market changes as plant closures, mergers, early retirement
incentives, and corporate downsizing. Advertising and marketing also
contribute to the persistence of this trend, as retirees are aggressively
courted on behalf of the housing, financial, clothing, travel, leisure, and
publishing industries.[1]

As this new concept of retirement has become normative, researchers
and scholars have begun to study it extensively and to map its unknown
territory. In general, research on the psychology of retirement seems to
divide on one major issue: While some psychologists see retirement as
a stressful life event, others view it as a normal life transition.

For those who view retirement as stressful, the reason for the stress is loss of something important in life, that is, one's job. The original loss may cause physical and emotional stresses related to grief. (For example, as detailed in chapter 9, retirement may trigger not only financial loss but also losses of status, activity, and identity that were previously provided by one's work.) According to the book *Everyday Psychologist*, some other factors that may accompany retirement or cause a stressful reaction include the following:

Pressure by others to retire

Spouse began or stopped work

Change in financial status

Taking on a part-time or volunteer job

Encountering legal problems

One or more children leaving home

Increase in eating, drinking, or smoking habits

Onset of serious illness or injury

Divorce or separation

Marriage or remarriage

Change of residence

Illness or death of spouse

Illness or death of close family member

Illness or death of close friend[2]

A second, much more positive way to regard retirement is to see it not as a life crisis but as a normal life transition. You simply move from one accepted stage or role in life to another, and the new stage gives you the gift of increased leisure time. According to this scenario, the major life task (not always a simple one) is the challenge to find substitute activities to give meaning to your life. This is a challenge we will explore further in chapter 4.

Both schools of thought on retirement agree that emotional adjustment to retirement is crucial. This may be difficult in the first year or two, when the retiree typically goes through five distinct phases: (1) preretirement, (2) honeymoon, (3) disenchantment, (4) reorientation, and (5) stability.[3] Please note that not every retiree goes through all five stages. Some skip one or more stages, whereas others (probably those who willingly and eagerly chose their retirement) are able to bypass the first four and settle happily in stability. But on the chance you may be one of the large number of retirees who will explore each stage, read on.

STAGE 1: PRERETIREMENT

Typically, new retirees experience deep anxiety about retirement and the changes it brings. They also fear losing their roles and status in society. Therefore, as retirement comes closer, their awareness moves into tentative acceptance and a time of eager or anxious fantasies about retirement, when the future will be either easy and playful or a downhill slide toward death. For most of us, preretirement acts as a kind of wake-up call to focus on health, income, and daily life. The task during this stage is to take advantage of the opportunity to begin to prepare emotionally and spiritually for a major life change.

STAGE 2: HONEYMOON

The second stage of retirement is the euphoric and sometimes frantic period when the new retiree tries to do everything at once—"all the things I never had time for." Like the marathon runner who starts with a burst of energy, instead of saving it for the long journey ahead, the new retiree can suffer from poor pacing. Not only is this a major cause of burnout, but it can also lead to neglect activities and roles that nourish the soul. Though it seems hard to believe, you *can* actually burn yourself out having a good time. Throwing yourself mindlessly into each new activity or blindly responding to everything that presents itself not only exhausts you but can burn out your spouse as well. The tasks in the honeymoon phase are to discover what parts of one's life need to be changed, sustained, or enhanced. Just as in the honeymoon of any relationship, the initial giddy delight soon yields to down-to-earth planning and grounded behavior that will provide long-term sustenance. The end of the honeymoon phase is marked by a more deliberate approach to how you spend your time and energy. Important strategies during this stage of retirement are to pace yourself and plan for the future.

STAGE 3: DISENCHANTMENT

The more unrealistic the dreams and fantasies of the preretirement and honeymoon stages, the more likely that disenchantment, and even depression, will sink in afterward. Life beyond the honeymoon is likely to feel a bit empty and anticlimactic. If you become absorbed in only one activity or relationship, you are at risk of depression if that activity or relationship disappears or lets you down. It's important to diversify, not only in terms of your financial portfolio but also in terms of your investments in emotional relationships and activities. The tasks in this stage of retirement include adjusting to new rhythms and pacing and reflecting on the realities of your new life. Those unable to complete these tasks may become stuck in this stage and mired in an unfulfilling, stagnating, even frightening retirement. However, if you can adjust and diversify successfully, this stage can help you reinvent yourself.

STAGE 4: REORIENTATION

During this stage, as you begin to reflect on your options, you can set realistic expectations for yourself. Reorientation can lead to a more active development of ideas and movement toward a more balanced and diversified set of actions, relationships, and routines. This stage is marked by determination to set and shape retirement goals in a direction that is pleasing. The tasks here are to establish who you are, how you want to live, and what you want to accomplish now.

STAGE 5: STABILITY

This stage is your actual retirement. It begins with your determination to live your life a certain way and is marked by a sense of exploration and adventure—a willingness either to experiment with new activities, interests, roles, and relationships or to remain comfortable with your current status quo. When you feel comfortable in your retirement, you've reached stability in your retired life. The tasks of this stage are to determine *for yourself* (outside of the pressures and expectations of family, friends, job, and community) who you want to be, what you want to do, and how you want to do it. This is, of course, no simple task. Those who achieve stability know what is expected of them, what is available to them, and what they need to do to remain satisfied and content.

Please note that these five stages are variable. There is no specific moment when one ends and the next begins. Some retirees, in fact, pass through each stage in days, weeks, or perhaps a month or two. Others may remain bogged down in one stage for years (particularly stage 3, disenchantment). Moreover, feelings and issues from an earlier stage may return as moods and concerns shift over time. The important thing to remember is that these five stages are normal and even necessary passages to a successful, happy retirement.

It might be useful right now to locate yourself within the five stages of retirement and notice the appropriate tasks for that stage. Where are you now? What should you be doing now? You might begin by assessing your greatest emotional concerns as you face retirement so that you can sort out your priorities.

The following list offers a starting point, plus references to the chapters in this book that discuss particular issues.

As I approach retirement, I'm most concerned about:

Fear of being cut off from social contact (chapter 8)

Feeling useless without career or job (chapters 4, 8)

Wondering if I should move or not (chapters 2, 3)

Boredom (chapters 4, 10)

Fear of not being able to make new friends (chapters 8, 11)

Adjustments with my spouse (chapter 6)

Finding new interests outside my career (chapters 4, 7)

Finding that I hate retirement (chapters 11, 12)

Becoming stagnant in retirement (chapters 4, 7, 12, 14)

Fears of aging and death (chapter 13)

As you can see, being retired becomes a career in itself, with its own tasks that require serious thought. It's a career that offers challenge, excitement, significant social contact, and great personal responsibility. In a sense, then, retiring is entering a whole new life.

TRANSITIONING FROM WORK TO RETIREMENT

Coming to terms with the various psychological and social changes that are part of the process of retirement is crucial. As you enter this new stage of life, you'll need to discover what it means to you (and your spouse or partner) to leave a full-time job and have unstructured time. Learning about these changes—and simply realizing that they will occur and are a normal part of the life process—can help you prepare to deal with them. Although change is usually difficult, it presents an opportunity for you to grow and develop into what you want to become. Retirement, like all the other life stages that precede it, is a highly dynamic period of life in which change is likely to happen.

As we recall from chapter 2, work plays a central role in most people's lives. It provides many or all of the following benefits:

Financial stability

Time management

Sense of purpose

Social life

Status, identity, and recognition

Source of power and influence

To get an idea of just how important work is to you, see which of the following statements describes you:

I place great importance on my work.

I think about work most of the time, even when I am home.

I feel I am indispensable to my company or business.

I place my work before my family, friends, and leisure time.

I look forward to each new workweek.

I dread the end of each workweek.

If you answered yes to most of these questions, you may identify very strongly with your own work identity and have a problem retiring. In fact, for you, work may be one of your strongest and best sources of joy and fulfillment.

Consider first what has attracted you to your particular work or career all these years. The following list represents the answers of well over 6,000 preretirees (from the survey, *Facts about Retiring in the United States*):

Feeling challenged by my work

Liking the people I work with

Having the opportunity to learn

Traveling for the company

Working as a team member

Helping the company grow

Being part of a respected company

Receiving the income and benefits

Influencing the company's direction and success[4]

If you would agree with this list (or at least most of the items on it), work is central to your life, and you need to realize that and plan for its loss and replacement. Use this information and your listing of work values as a planning tool to help you decide what to do in retirement. Remember that people do not usually change their personality or values in retirement; these values remain rather constant throughout life. Examine the preceding list again and decide which items on that list you will miss. Then begin to think about what you might do to replace them.

Moreover, there are other reasons why you might find your transition into retirement extremely difficult. Here are some additional possibilities:

1. *Retirement is new and uncharted territory for you.* As a competent, working adult, you knew what to do at work each day and more or less what to expect. Standards and practices were probably well defined and publicized. Success was concrete and measurable, as was feedback. You knew when you were on track and when you weren't! There were almost always *external* factors available to help you measure your success.

   In contrast, the entire retirement process is motivated and measured from *within*. You must set your own goals and standards and decide for yourself whether or not you are meeting them. You also must decide on what constitutes meaningful activity for yourself and then evaluate your own progress. There are few outside standards or guidelines; you are the chief executive officer of your own retirement.

2. *Retirement will move you into unknown areas.* The unknown is almost always uncomfortable territory. You're entering a new realm, and you may not have had time in your busy work life to prepare. Most human beings fear change and many of us are terrified of dwelling in unfamiliar territory.

3. *You will probably feel a sense of loss.* It is normal to worry about losing your friends at work, along with the sense of purpose and participation in something larger than yourself that guided your working days. For many people, it's difficult to acknowledge, let alone discuss, the significant loss of power, prestige, and influence you will experience. Moreover, your transition to retirement will be even harder if you have been unaware of these possible losses and therefore have no ideas or plans to compensate for them.

4. *You may be caught by surprise with an offer of early retirement.* You may not even have thought of retirement, and might even have been plan-

ning to work for your company for several more years. You may have been shocked by the sudden offer of early retirement. What can you do? You need to consider several questions before deciding on your answer:

- Do you want to retire?
- Can you afford to retire?
- What will you do with your time?
- If you really don't want to retire, what are the consequences of turning down the offer?
- Will your department be phased out?
- Will your job change?
- Would you be demoted or downsized?
- Will you be able to receive as much in the *next* early retirement package if you turn down this one?

These are difficult but important questions to answer. Unfortunately you may have to make your best guess as to the answers; the information in hard form may not be available to you.

Moreover, retirement is not only a career but also a *process*. Erik Erikson, the eminent psychologist, described the tasks of later adulthood as accepting one's accomplishments and failures, resolving old issues, and facing fully the reality of one's entire life.[5] He felt that you either succeed in this ability to accept your life and lead it to the fullest or succumb to stagnation and ultimately to despair.

When you reach the stability stage of your retirement, you achieve the integrity and acceptance that Erikson describes. Having worked through the emotional and spiritual questions of the first four stages, you enter into the wonderful period in which retirement becomes truly an opportunity: the gift of free time that you can choose to convert into self-fulfillment.

Points to Remember

- Knowledge of the five stages of retirement (preretirement, honeymoon, disenchantment, reorientation, and stability) helps to ward off stress.
- Assess and plan for your areas of concern *before* you retire.

NOTES

1. This trend is discussed more fully in the introductory section of Savishinsky's *Breaking the Watch*.

2. *The Everyday Psychologist*, 32–36.

3. These five stages are discussed in Phil Rich, Dorothy Sampson, and Dale Fetherling's *The Healing Journey Through Retirement*, 17–23.

4. Steven Shagrin, ed., *Facts about Retiring in the United States*.

5. Erikson's thoughts are summarized and paraphrased in Evelyn Eaton Whitehead and James D. Whitehead, *Christian Life Patterns*, 135–51. They are also discussed more fully in chapter 13 of this book.

4

———∞∞∞———

But What Will I Do All Day?:
Structuring Your Time

Life begets life. Energy creates energy. It is only by spending oneself
that one becomes rich.

> —Sarah Bernhardt

You cannot kill time without injuring eternity.

> —H. D. Thoreau

The question posed by this chapter is the one that bedevils many retirees. Envisioning an endless stretch of empty days ahead—identical, pur-
poseless, and punctuated only by the morning paper and the evening
news on TV—some retirees actually panic. In fact, for most people an-
ticipating retirement, the issue of structure and purpose is probably the
second-greatest fear factor (after loss of financial security).

For the retirees in my survey, however, it turned out that time was
not much of a problem. Let's see if what they discovered can be helpful.

One respondent confessed that:

> It's a work in progress. But at present it's a combination of writing, board
> work, travel, and fun.

Another respondent structures her time for balance:

> Ideal—one-third personal (includes health, fitness); one-third community
> work; one-third family (includes travel).

One retired man told me:

I love being involved in what I'm doing. I try to structure my time for balance, but to be flexible and adaptable.

And a retired dentist expressed similar feelings:

I try to balance the spiritual, social, and financial aspects of retirement. I am active in the community. Have served on the condo board of directors for the past five years and have been president the past three years. . . . I am as busy as I want to be.

For most women retirees, life is comprised of volunteer commitment, time at home, travel, and exercise, while many maintain a careful balancing act:

The difficulty is finding meaningful activities that don't impinge on the new freedom and spontaneity. Commitment on your own terms and schedule.

This respondent's husband, also retired, adds:

Try to keep a balance between other-directed and inner-directed goals and needs. Make sure to keep good friends and make new ones. Put in enough structure to avoid drifting, [yet] not so much that you lose spontaneous pleasures.

Another woman confesses:

I always plan at least one activity a day outside the house. I also continue to keep a to-do list of things I need to accomplish.

And she goes on to admit that:

The biggest adjustment was the concept of time. When working, there was never enough time—my entire life was on schedule. Even after two years, I often forget that I have time to do things that I didn't "schedule" or go off to explore new places or ideas.

A retired nun comments on her balancing act:

At times I feel I have taken on too much—at other times I feel I don't have enough to do—I keep seeking balance. . . . I endeavor to have a definite plan for each weekday morning—not too rigid or rushed but definitely planned. And I always have a "to do" and a "wish" list. . . . I'll probably die with a list of "yet to do's"—and I hope I do!

What we learn from successful retirees is that deciding and creating a purpose for their own retirement yields just about as much (or as little) structure as they need or want. Once you've grappled with the purpose of your retirement (as you will in chapter 9), meaning emerges naturally, and the days seem to fall easily into place. As Richard Johnson explains:

> Retirement gives us the forum in which our search for meaning can play out in ways only dreamed about in our former lifestyle. . . . Those who venture into retirement unenlightened risk their new and undefined lifestyle becoming a challenge to their self-esteem rather than realizing it as a life-enhancer and self-affirmer they had supposed it to be.[1]

Our enlightened retirees had already come to terms with who they were and what they wanted their retirement to look like. Clearly, the amount of activity and structure needed for life satisfaction varies from person to person, and one man's ideal retirement would send another around the bend in frustration. Here again, one size does *not* fit all.

What becomes clear is that successful retirees have asked themselves (and answered) the following lifestyle questions:

> What do you *want* to do?
> What do you enjoy doing?
> What are you able to do?
> What do you believe is important?

That last question introduces the concept of personal values, which is next in importance to purpose in determining the structure of your retirement life (and which we will discuss in chapter 8). Now, let's explore the idea of values further.

There are several ways to arrive at discovering your own values and motivation, but one of the most important (and underused) tools is fantasy. Fantasy transforms us and gives us the magical power to aspire. Boston writer Linda Weltner amusingly describes a transforming fantasy experienced by her husband Jack as he prepared to retire:

> My husband had his eye on golf. Three years ago—at age sixty-four—he was planning his retirement and his life on the golf course, when a friend gave him as a birthday gift a psychic reading with a woman named Louisa

Poole. . . . My husband came back, dazed to the core and informed me that he was a Boddhi Satva [sic]. Let me tell you, I don't wish on any of you the prospect of your husband walking in the door and telling you that he is actually a perfected being . . . who was reborn because he had a crucial mission to accomplish before he died.

Talk about a wild fantasy! . . . Louisa had told him that his mission would begin at sixty-five, and would completely take up the last part of his life. Imagine, if you can, my husband asking all his friends if they had any idea what his mission was. He behaved as if he were on a scavenger hunt and his mission had been hidden by someone behind the bushes.

But when no one could provide an answer, he came up with one himself. He was already working at the Lynn Community Health Center as a part-time psychiatrist, because he wanted to make a contribution to those less fortunate. But within a year, he had instituted a training program for local universities in psychiatric nursing, opened a walk-in clinic, and recruited a dozen volunteers. Three years after his fantastic prophecy, he was nominated "Compassionate Caretaker of the Year." . . . He has never worked harder or longer or more passionately. [2]

Linda asks whether the psychic *caused* the transformation of a gullible man or if something else happened.

Her prophecy took something already in Jack's life, his work at the clinic, and transformed it into a mission. His fantasy made what had previously been an ordinary undertaking into something foreordained and miraculous. It ignited energy that had been flagging, took a well-meaning, highly competent doctor and turned him into someone extraordinary. . . . Louisa Poole, I think, gave Jack permission to have delusions of grandeur. And he made them real. [3]

Retirement is, of course, when we are free to indulge "delusions of grandeur" and make them real. Discovery of our own meaning and mission is like happiness. It's an inside job. We might ask a psychic to predict our mission, but it is always ours to choose.

We begin by asking ourselves the values questions posed at the end of the previous chapter. What activities do you see yourself moving away from? Where are you headed?

Another way of looking at this task is to ask yourself what you would like to include in your retirement life. For one survey respondent, the answers generated a slew of activities (volunteering, computer courses, bridge lessons, and Italian classes) and also the realization of what she did not want to pursue: "Along the way I recognized that I would never go back to playing the piano!"

For a semiretired surgeon looking ahead to retirement, the answer to that question included a detailed list of activities in a five-year plan:

Continue to practice medicine.

Direct Institute fundraising efforts and vision.

Increase business activities.

Write, lecture, and study.

Create time to improve and create relationships with family and friends.

Improve my health, body strength, and spiritual well-being.

Before you begin to structure the specifics of your retirement, it might be useful to pause and think seriously about exactly what you want to include in your life during retirement. By the time you retire, you will probably already be involved in (if not immersed in) a number of worthwhile (or perhaps not so worthwhile) activities. Begin your planning simply by listing the things you are currently involved in. Next, make a separate list headed, "Things I Want to Do but Am Not Doing/Not Doing Enough Of."

Sarah, a recently retired executive in my survey, began her retirement planning by creating such a list. With her permission, I include it here. She started with four activities that she wanted either to begin or increase during her retirement:

1. Exercise
2. Study
3. Planning
4. Learning

Next, she modified her initial list by adding specifics under her four general headings.

1. Exercise:

   Gym
   Hiking

2. Study:

   Investments
   Spanish

3. Planning:

Time management
Garden maintenance

4. Learning:

Computer
Spanish conversation

Once she established her overall life-planning goals, Sarah asked (and continued to ask) the following basic questions regarding her planned activities:

What am I doing with my life now?
What are the benefits and costs of doing it?
Is doing this providing me with what I want?
Am I accomplishing my purpose?
If not, can I change what I'm doing to better accommodate my purpose?

Another way for Sarah to look at her life-planning goals is to group under the life categories all the activities that she wants to include under each subheading. For example, her six subheadings include health, marriage, family, community boards and committees, friends, and self. The activities Sarah added to the headings produced the list:

1. Health:

Treadmill, walk, bike
Garden
Weights
Diet, vitamins
Massage, stretch

2. Marriage:

Health
Study, current events
Social life, travel, activities

3. Family:

Shared activities, events

4. Community boards and committees:

Symphony orchestra board
Art society

Garden club board
Condominium board

5. Friends:

Shared activities

6. Self:

Do meaningful work
Feel valued because of contribution
Keep mentally stimulated

Sarah then created a form to help her identify those activities and interests she wanted to include in retirement, as well as a method for clarifying the value and satisfaction each one affords her. Again, with her permission I include a sample of her Retirement Life Grid, plus a blank form for you to use in planning your own.

EDUCATION: USE IT OR LOSE IT

As we will learn in chapter 8, continuing your education is one of your most valuable retirement resources. Most of us look back wistfully on our college and high school days as "among the best of our lives" and even wish we could have had a longer period to engage in systematic learning, free of midlife responsibilities. Once you are in retirement, you will have plenty of time to learn new things. And yet, few retirees actually engage in such programs. Why don't they?

Although no one knows why some older people seem resistant to learning, evidence is accumulating[4] that it has a great deal to do with how we use or underuse our brain throughout our life. The old saying, "Use it or lose it," seems to apply to exercising the mind as well as the body. A brain that is not challenged to learn new things for an extended period in the present will actually become smaller and less capable of learning in the future.

According to researchers quoted in the January 1, 2000, issue of *Newsweek*, "You create your brain from the input you get." With this in mind, it's easy to see that continuing to be an active learner throughout life may contribute to both a healthier brain and less boredom during retirement. Moreover, the important thing is to become actively involved in areas unfamiliar to you. It's best to challenge yourself to learn a *new* subject. For example, if you are already fluent in two languages, try learning a musical instrument, solving crossword puzzles, or mastering the computer. Moreover, group-learning situations offer a perfect setting

Table 4.1
Sample Retirement Life Grid

Activity	Time (hours per month)	Benefit	Related to Life Purpose/Plan
Study Spanish	4 hours	• intellectual exercise • fun in Spain	yes
Symphony board	2 hours	• socialization • feeling of self-worth • practice thinking about investments	yes
Art society	3 hours	• socialization • feeling of self-worth • learn new skills • satisfaction/work for parks	yes
Garden club	3 hours	• socialization • belonging	yes
Women's stock club investment committee	½ hour	• socialization • intellectual stimulation	yes
Exercise with trainer	4 hours	• health, learning	yes
Private exercise or health club	10 hours	• health • socialization	yes
Mail/desk work	13 hours	• organization • administration	√ necessary maintenance
Household management	8 hours	• organization • administration	√ necessary maintenance

for socializing. Retirement offers the ideal opportunity to challenge your mind with new learning.[5]

Like travel, learning opens up new worlds, shows us places we've never been, and teaches us new ways of thinking. It makes us feel rejuvenated, because knowledge is newness in its purest form.

For retirees, the impulse to learn is a natural outcome of the "growth spurt" of late middle age. ("If I'm learning, I'm growing, and if I'm growing, I'm still alive.") The idea of following wherever curiosity leads, of exploring new ideas, fills the void that opened up when we left our old job. Now is the time to pursue that lifelong interest you always wanted

Table 4.2
Your Retirement Life Grid Form

Activity	Time (hours per month)	Benefit	Related to Life Purpose/Plan

to develop. "I grow old learning something new every day," said Solon, the Athenian statesman. He had nothing on today's eager retirement scholars.

DO WELL BY DOING GOOD: VOLUNTEERING

A study by the U.S. government's foster grandparent and senior companion programs concluded that

> In addition to evidence that seniors can contribute in important ways through service, there are indications that the seniors greatly benefit themselves by serving. In fact, the engine driving senior service may well be less airy altruism than a strong and straightforward desire for structure, purpose, affiliation, growth and meaning.[6]

Research indicated that the volunteer participants' mental health and social resources improved over three years, while those on the waiting list to become foster grandparents actually declined in three areas. Indeed, 71 percent of the foster grandparents reported that they "almost never" felt lonely (compared with 45 percent of the waiting-list group), and 83 percent reported being "more satisfied with their life" (compared to 52 percent of those on the waiting list). Volunteering for a good cause seems to provide the same benefits that work does in the private sector (minus the paycheck, of course). In fact, in terms of providing structure, discipline, and activity in one's life, volunteering fills the bill. And it becomes even more important to those whose preretirement jobs were not fulfilling to them. Retirees can often become involved as volunteers at higher levels of an agency or nonprofit institution and influence it in ways that were unreachable while they were working.

There are five other reasons why working as a volunteer can prove even more satisfying that "regular" paid work:

1. *Doing interesting work.* Nonprofits allow you to pursue fascinating activities that suit your capabilities.
2. *Looking to the future.* Making the world better seems to offset the inevitability of death. Or, as psychologist Erik Erikson put it, "I am what survives me."
3. *Paying back society.* Working with nonprofits helps us pass on the love and support once given us. This is our "rent" payment for our space on earth.

4. *Meeting interesting people*. Covolunteers at nonprofits share your interests and passion.

5. *Staying active*. Nonprofits do not discard their veterans, as for-profit companies often do.

Just as it is important to prepare for a job in the private sector, planning ahead can be key to succeeding as a volunteer.

1. Make sure you do your homework on a prospective volunteer agency.

2. Brush up on the skills you can bring to the agency.

3. To make your volunteering a pleasant experience, scrutinize the commitment with the same critical eye you would use to assess a paying job.

4. Interview the agency as carefully as you interviewed for your paying jobs.

5. Make sure that you have found a good fit for your abilities and interests. Instead of just taking anything available, explain to the agency what you can bring them and what you can and want to do.

HOW TO VOLUNTEER

In deciding where to volunteer, use as much care and attention as you did in choosing your career. Don't just take the first available opening; review your own needs and desires first. Your first question should be, "What do I really care about?" Begin with a category (health, children, women's issues, the environment) and within that category, ask yourself what area you wish to become involved in (advocacy, board work, hands-on delivery of service, one-on-one interaction). Then ask yourself how much time you can give to volunteer work.

In the first flush of leisure after retirement, you may be tempted to commit to several causes and become overextended. Pick one or two at first and begin slowly, giving a little of your time and effort to each before fully committing to anything. One of the best things about volunteering is that you get to decide just where, how often, and how long you want to work.

The last question to ask yourself is, "What can I do for this cause or organization?" Here you have another choice. After inventorying your skills, you can continue to do the kind of work you did previously in your job (e.g., accounting, publicity, or nursing), only now you will do it for free. Or you can be more adventurous and attempt to employ skills you haven't used before or haven't had time to develop (fundraising, event planning, computer skills). Either way you choose, you will be benefiting others while you fulfill your own needs.

For information on volunteer opportunities, consult your local newspaper, the United Way/Community Chest in your area, your local Retired Senior Volunteer Program (RSVP), or your local Volunteer Action Council. Another good spot to look is at your place of worship. Most churches have their own programs and are happy to match volunteers with their own or other community programs.

There is a comprehensive Web site that's perfect if you're not sure where to volunteer or how much you want to get involved. Called Volunteer Match (www.volunteermatch.org), it lists volunteer opportunities that have been requested by nonprofits in your own area. You search by zip code. These opportunities can be one-time events or ongoing opportunities, so you can pick according to your skills and time available.

Also be alert to attempting new activities outside your comfort zone. Volunteering in retirement gives you the chance to try out ideas and try on new skills—perhaps in community theater or art therapy. Your level of skill is not as important as your desire to bring something of value to others' lives. The benefits—to you as well as to others—will be considerable.

People who work to improve the world, or at least their own little corner of it, seem to keep a sense of vitality that is missing in those who tend to become intensely self-absorbed. Whatever your "cause"—environment, health, education, community service, justice, or the arts—volunteering gives a sparkle to the eye and a spring to the step, for it keeps you vitally participating in the world. (My own mother is a prime example. A lifelong volunteer, she is still actively volunteering at a care facility at age 95.) We must not forget the bonus of volunteer work, which is the opportunity to meet new people and make new friends. As Sharon, a retired nurse who volunteers, wrote:

> The more involved I am, the more interested in life I am. The more interested, the more learning takes place in me. The more "smarts" I get, the more need to participate. . . . I've been given a great deal in my life. Now it's my turn to give back.

If you're ready to start volunteering your time, answering the following questions can help you to clarify what you want to do, with what group, and how much time you want to commit:

1. Do you *want* to volunteer your time?

2. What sort of personal gains do you think you might acquire from volunteering?

3. How could the community benefit from your volunteer work?

4. What sort of volunteer work would you like to do? In what setting?

5. Ideally, how much time are you willing to commit? How flexible (or seasonally available) will you be?

6. Who do you know who could introduce you to this activity?

USES OF LEISURE

Leisure (loosely defined as what you do when you don't have to do anything else) is the centerpiece of most retirees' daydreams of the future. At the same time, it is often a misunderstood aspect of retirement; one person's leisure is another's work. Leisure is both a universal desire and a fundamental need of human beings. Leisure can include social interaction (parties, visits), spectator appreciation (sports, travel), creative expression (writing, photography, painting), mental stimulation (reading, visiting museums, attending lectures, collecting), physical exercise (sports, yoga), and solitary relaxation (reading, listening to music). It is all a matter of your own taste.

And yet, like work, leisure can be the means to develop feelings of self-worth, social status, and individual potential. Leisure activities can improve physical health, enhance emotional well being, expand social interaction, and help us find meaningful roles in life. Retirees who expressed the most satisfaction with life are the same people who already generated specific leisure interests before they retired and were already pursuing them with gusto.

However, as important as leisure is in retirement, it cannot become the central focus of life. When leisure becomes the main thrust of our life, it ceases to bring us the benefits we need from it. Leisure is a "break," a little vacation from real life, not the main event. Paradoxically, in order to be a diversion, leisure must be confined to our leisure time. Many a retiree has planned "to fish" during retirement, only to find that daily preoccupation with fishing makes it just another task to perform and, ultimately, a boring job. Leisure activities are the icing on the cake, not the cake itself. As one of my respondents put it:

> Even the most enjoyable activities can become onerous if they are too structured or planned. . . . Just enjoy it—if you have to work hard at it maybe you should go back to work.

Too much leisure can thus be as deadly as too much work. As George Bernard Shaw observed, "The secret of being miserable is to have the leisure to bother about whether you are happy or not."

One of the happiest and best uses of leisure time is in the pursuit of hobbies. The dictionary defines a hobby as "something that a person likes to do in his spare time," which certainly covers a lot of ground!

For the retiree, hobbies—and having them—are literally priceless. Now is the chance to do all those interesting things you've always wanted to do but put off all your life. This is a great opportunity, but only if you already have hobbies or at least have plans to develop one or more in the near future. Test yourself now: outside of your work and family, can you name at least one truly fascinating activity on which you currently spend a significant amount of time?

If, like many adults, your answer is that you've never had time to either follow up on old interests or develop new ones, but you plan to do so after retirement, think again! You may risk having a difficult and even unhappy retirement. The reason is simple: very few people who have not discovered and cultivated real interests during their middle years are able to do so in their sixties, seventies, and eighties. As a result, many of these people end up bored and disappointed in their retirement, no matter what their income level. For too many retirees, the only hobby is television watching.

It's important to keep nurturing new interests (or at least renewing old ones) during the busy middle years in order to have something of interest after retirement. You will certainly have the time to develop and pursue new hobbies after retirement, but you may have lost the skill and curiosity to tap into your own creativity and ability. Just like a muscle, curiosity and the love of pursuing something interesting can atrophy with disuse.

How long has it been since you started a genuine new interest? And how long since you enjoyed an old one? If you can honestly say last week or last month, the chances are good you have nourished your curiosity and your interests and will have much to fall back on and to enjoy during retirement.

Remember your teenage years and early twenties? Probably you were interested in many activities, and tried all kinds of sports. But with aging and responsibilities, we often lose track of our early interests and let them drop. You might remember fondly when you climbed rocks, wrote poetry, or went sailing, but you may not feel so adventurous now.

Take a few moments now to think of all your former pastimes. Can you list any that still interest you? Remember, the possibilities for hobbies are almost endless. They can include any or all of the following:

Sports and games

Creative arts (poetry, music, painting, dance, singing, writing)

Culture (art, music, dance, architecture appreciation)

Crafts

Gardening or communing with nature

Collecting of any type of object

Adventure or wilderness experience

Past or former hobbies that still interest me or that I might like to pursue:

1. _____
2. _____
3. _____

If there are any former hobbies that you feel you are no longer interested in, please list them here, together with the reason you're no longer involved.

1. _____ because _____

_____

2. _____ because _____

_____

3. _____ because _____

_____

Your reasons for discarding them may surprise you—or you may want to reconsider them in the light of where you are today.

Now, list any activity that is new to you but that you'd really like to pursue when you have the time in retirement. Be brave here and include anything that fascinates you or that you think might interest you in the future:

1. _____
2. _____
3. _____

Make a concentrated effort to plan to pursue at least one of these activities during retirement. Better yet, begin your pursuit right now—don't wait. Particularly if you've ever thought of yourself as a creative person (e.g., a musician, a painter, a poet), make a real effort to rediscover or nurture those artistic impulses in retirement. Older artists often do well, experiencing bursts of creativity long after age 65. (Grandma Moses only began to paint in her seventies, and Picasso remained productive well into his nineties.) Artists and people with creative and craft interests seem to remain particularly vital and purposeful into old age, which speaks well for the value of a creative hobby.

The importance of hobbies, particularly for the retired person, is unmistakable. They provide a sense of purpose, time structure, and a sense of accomplishment and productivity, and they often give rise to a whole new circle of friends with like-minded interests. And, of course, delight is a powerful byproduct of pursuing a hobby. (In fact, you'll notice that hobbies supply almost all the needs formerly filled by work—except, of course, the paycheck!)

But if you wish, it's even possible to turn a beloved hobby into a paycheck. You can transform a hobby—for example, garden design—into a business. Of course, you'll have to know more than plant names and landscape design principles; you'll also need to master the skills of running a small business (marketing services, purchasing plants wholesale, hiring help, charging, billing, and collecting accounts).

Many retirees in my survey have found ways to turn their hobbies into profit: Mary Ann turned a talent for decorating unique birthday cakes into a thriving specialty, and supplied her cakes to bakeries; Mike developed his hobby of woodworking and carpentry into a renovation business; and Jean transformed her artistic eye and design abilities into a business providing unique baby clothes. For them, their hobbies offer not only the benefits of meaning, purpose, structure, and enjoyment but also valid sources of self-esteem and pride.

But profit is not the real purpose of hobbies—and turning your hobby into profit may rob some of its joy for you. Concentrate on the passion you find in your hobby and you will be on the right track. When we think of "hobby" we might think only of a pastime, literally something to fill time, but we rarely imagine it as a source of passion. Yet hobbies can indeed become passions, especially when two or more interests combine in new and unexpected ways.

Remember Mary, the widowed traveler from chapter 2? After she returned from her first African safari, she was so excited about her discovery of the animal kingdom that she began volunteering at her local zoo. At the same time, early in her retirement, she rekindled an old interest in photography. She pursued her two interests separately for many months until one day, someone at the zoo office mentioned that they needed a person to photograph the animals in preparation for a new publicity campaign. Mary volunteered, and her work was so well received that she was subsequently asked to photograph some of the zoo exhibits and animal habitats in connection with publicity materials for the zoo. Eventually, she became so well known locally as an animal photographer that she was invited to accompany the zoo director and a tour group on several zoo-sponsored safaris and adventure trips in order to photograph and document their travels. "I feel like I've come full circle," says Mary. "I am so grateful to have the opportunity to join my two interests—a new one in wildlife and my old hobby photography—in this way. It truly has become my passion."

One of the not-so-hidden benefits of hobbies is the fact that they often lead to new and deeper friendships and widen our network of companionship, something we need more of as we retire. America used to be a country of joiners—historically, we signed up for everything from church to garden clubs, the PTA, and the Moose Lodge. Recently, this strong natural proclivity to join groups seems to have declined.

In his landmark book *Bowling Alone: The Collapse and Revival of American Community*, Robert Putnam speculates that the main reasons for the reversal are:

- Women joining the labor force.
- People have less time to join anything.
- Mobility—which discourages civic and local involvement.
- Demographic transformations—including fewer marriages, more divorces, less real wages.
- The transformation of leisure—television, computers and other technological devices have privatized leisure. Rather than playing games with others, we watch TV.[7]

Whatever the reasons, most middle-aged Americans belong to fewer groups than they used to. Unfortunately, the implications of this for a nonjoiner's retirement years are not good; many people who retire in a few years will find that, without a job, they don't belong anywhere.

Here is where people with hobbies have another advantage. They automatically meet and socialize with a group interested in the same intellectual pursuits, sports, or passions that they share. And since these hobby groups are interest-driven, not age-limited, they have the added benefit of meeting and befriending stimulating new friends of all ages—including younger ones.

A retirement life in endless continuation of the same old activities can become a life of boredom, as well as one of limited meaning and growth. To stay interested—and interesting—after retirement, most of us will need to pursue at least several different interests. For example, you may want to hike in the morning and volunteer at a food bank for the homeless in the afternoon. But whatever you choose to do, it's key to keep expanding your options for activities and joining with others as you pursue them. The possibilities for meaningful hobbies and new friendships are endless if you look carefully.

THE HOBBY OF CREATIVITY

The most exciting possibilities of all in retirement are those that open up in discovering—or perhaps rediscovering—our creativity. The word "creativity" may seem a bit daunting, and most of us are not accustomed to thinking of ourselves in those terms. We think of creative people as poets, authors, actors, musicians, and artists and conclude that most of us simply don't qualify. But creativity really refers to making something (anything) new, to applying our own unique perspective and slant to familiar materials or experiences. Viewed that way, it's easy to see that we all have something within us that is creative, that deserves bringing to completion and sharing with others. Your creativity can be expressed in building shelves or a birdhouse, dressing in colorful and unique ways, designing and cooking a great meal, or throwing an exceptional party. Indeed, anything you do that is out of the ordinary and that releases a feeling of joy in being alive is creative.

And the good news is that it is never too late to become creative or even "artistic," if you have an open mind and a self-forgiving heart. Whatever you choose to do, do it for the sheer love of the activity and don't worry about how well you perform. You may have to lower your standards a bit in order to fulfill a lifelong desire to be creative! Remember, this is not about performing to someone else's standards or meeting artistic criteria; the goal is joyful self-expression. The enemies of joy in creativity are judgment and perfectionism. Of course you're going to face some limitations and will probably never perform to professional standards, but so what? The joys of creativity and the satisfaction that comes from real self-expression should outweigh any fear or limitation.

Don't forget that being an audience is an important part of creative expression. The appreciator of art is also a creative participant in the arts. The artist's work represents one-half of the equation; he needs someone to receive and appreciate the finished creation. In fact, art is fed creatively by appreciation and response. Attending plays and concerts, visiting galleries, and listening to lectures are all creative endeavors.

Creativity is a two-way street and at some level is present in all of us. In discovering our own creativity, we open ourselves to one of the most satisfying pursuits of our retirement.

PART-TIME WORK

A Louis Harris survey reports that 78 percent of those 65 and older in the labor force prefer to continue working at least part time after the traditional retirement age. Retirees who miss the hustle and bustle of their old jobs and work part time find it to be an opportunity to stay involved with life and business on a reduced schedule. In addition, working a few extra years beyond retirement age can help ease financial burdens. But for most people, money is not the main motivation for part-time work. They enjoy the intellectual stimulation, social interactions, and, most importantly, the sense of purpose that accompanies having a job.

According to a 1998 survey by the American Association of Retired Persons (AARP), 80 percent of workers in the baby boom generation look forward to engaging in at least part-time work after they retire. However, in spite of federal anti–age discrimination acts, such as the ADEA, it's one thing to look forward to working and another thing to actually obtain a part-time job over age 65.

If you hope to be one of the lucky ones and want more than a minimum wage job, it's a good idea to plan well in advance. Your new job, while not necessarily in your current or former field, should make good use of the skills you already have or those you can obtain fairly easily with additional training. Try to get some hands-on experience in your new field (teaching, working in a plant nursery, consulting, or caring for small children) before you retire to see if you find it satisfying.

For example, if you plan to sell your successful small business and go into part-time consulting in the same field, before you take the plunge, you might need to develop or hone some of your skills, including improving your writing ability, learning to use the computer, and learning cost-effective marketing strategies. One good approach is to arrange to work with someone who is already successfully running a consulting business.

In fact, anyone who wants to turn a hobby into a part-time business will have to learn how to master small business skills, including marketing, purchasing, hiring employees, billing, and bookkeeping.

The questions to ask yourself as you think about returning to work (part time or full time) are these (You might want to take the time to answer them now, in a notebook):

1. Do you want to return to work or develop your own business?

2. If so, why? Be as specific as possible. (What would you gain or lose?)

3. If you return, how much time do you want to spend on your job?

4. Are you more interested in a job or in owning your own business?

5. If money is *not* a motivator, would volunteer work provide the rewards you seek?

6. What kind of work do you prefer?

7. What job-related skills do you have? List them here, and don't be modest.

8. What jobs or work have you always wanted to try?

9. What special interests, training, or hobbies do you have that you might incorporate into a new business?

10. Looking back on all these answers, what sort of work or business do you most want to be involved in?

Now you can begin to "connect the dots" suggested by your answers and narrow down your choices. For example, if you really like pets, are an energetic self-starter who is free to work irregular hours or days, and who doesn't want the office grind, you might consider working part time at a pet store. If you want to own a business, you might start your own pet store, buy an existing one, or start a pet-sitting or pet exercise service. The possibilities are there if you look for them.

One advantage of working part time is that it can bridge the gap between full retirement and staying pleasantly busy. Many such jobs exist in the service industry (churches, schools, hotels, restaurants, and libraries), where the pay is less but the time demands are also less.

Seasonal work (pre-Christmas, tax season, summer work in camps and resorts) is another possibility, as is registering with a temporary employment agency. Other work lending itself to part-time work for independent people includes sales and real estate, for which a license (and evening and weekend work) is required.

One of my respondents, Lois (who we will meet again in chapter 5), timed her retirement carefully, and then made sure that she transitioned well into a part-time consulting position during her retirement:

> I gave my employer six months' notice so that we could both plan successfully. We agreed that we would both benefit if I continued to be involved with the agency as a "consultant." As a result I continue to do some paid work from a dedicated office in my home. A quarter or less of my time is spent working either for the agency or other clients who are referred by graphic artists, etcetera. I like being able to "keep my hand in" the marketing business. It keeps me abreast of what's happening in the community.

She also makes sure that she includes a desired balance of activities and leisure in her life plan:

> Another quarter of my time is spent in community work. I have chosen this aspect very carefully. I prefer to be involved in hands-on projects that utilize the skills I honed in my professional life. I am involved with three organizations: Radio Reading Services (Association for the Blind), the Youth Collaborative, and the Interfaith Hospitality Network. The first two organizations tap directly into skills acquired as an English teacher for 22 years; the latter utilizes the marketing and public relations knowledge from a dozen years with an advertising agency. The remainder of the time is for family, friends, and myself. I have time to do things during the day now such as lunching with friends, exercising before breakfast, reading, gardening during the week, and so on.

Dr. Eben Alexander, in a humorous yet profound article about retiring from a position of authority but remaining an employee of an institution, gives some excellent advice on retiring gracefully while remaining with the company. Among his suggestions are:

1. Recognize your successor's authority. . . . You have had your years to make an imprint as leader, and you must accept that that part of your life is over.
2. Retain a low profile—definitely a lesson in humility.
3. Restructure your relationships carefully at work: retaining the old relationships can be a serious source of division. No one benefits from displaced loyalties.

And these final points, which are appropriate to *all* older workers:

4. Assume you are going to live at least ten more years and make every moment count, every relationship a happy one, and every task a privilege. Be glad that you are alive and still able to contribute to your chosen field.

5. Do not talk about "the good old days" unless specifically asked to do so. Think and talk about the present and the future instead.[8]

Whatever you choose, remember the paradoxical words of the nineteenth-century essayist, William Hazlitt:

"The more we do, the more we can do; the busier we are, the more leisure we have."

THE FINAL RECOMMENDATION

The ultimate answer to the question posed by this chapter is, like everything else in the book, up to you. Only you can decide how much structure you need or desire. Only you can decide whether the balance of your days will be tipped in favor of education, travel, volunteering, leisure activities, full- or part-time work, or in some combination of these. The solution is to find what really motivates you and be committed to it. For many high-powered Type A retirees, for example, the best way to "retire" is to continue working at something. Identify a work environment—a community activity, a small company, or a family or household project—that allows you to use your skills and tap into your interests. If you volunteer or begin a part-time job, make sure the environment fits your personality and values your work style. Even if you set up a home office, begin to work in your work environment, and keep regular hours to work on your project or activity. Take as much time as you need to find the right environment and the right balance of leisure and meaningful activity. See the adjustment to retirement as a challenge, one to which you are fully committed. Remember the words of a successful retiree who insists: "I love not working. But it helps to have a passion—something you love and can indulge."

As one of my respondents noted:

The key is having choices/options so that decisions can be made on the basis of what one wants to do—not has to do. . . . What is crucial however, is how one handles challenges (unexpected illness, death, disappointment) because we will all be required to face these situations. Sometimes it's not about what one wants to do but what one has to do that determines a life. . . . Retirement is a gift of time—but its real burden is the terrible—and wonderful—gift of freedom and its own responsibilities.

Points to Remember

- The amount of structured time in retirement is a matter of individual preference and need.
- Personal values determine the balance between "doing" and "being" in retirement.
- Creating your own "Retirement Life Grid" can be helpful in sorting your priorities and assessing the value of various activities.
- Education, volunteer work, part-time work, travel, and enjoyment of leisure are significant elements of a happy retirement.

NOTES

1. Johnson, *Creating a Successful Retirement*, 63–64.

2. Linda Weltner, "Fantasy Energizes Daily Life." Lecture given at Harvard Divinity School, 22 March 2001 and reprinted as a pamphlet by Roundtable Press, Wellesley, Mass., 2001.

3. Weltner, 3.

4. Warner, 30–31.

5. Sharon Begley with Erica Check, "Rewiring Your Gray Matter," *Newsweek*, 1 January 2000, 64.

6. Quoted by Warner, 23.

7. Robert Putnam, *Bowling Alone: The Collapse and Revival of American Community.*

8. Alexander, 19.

5

—∞∞∞—

Looking in the Mirror:
Self-Image in Retirement

Man desires to be free and he desires to be important. This places him in a dilemma, for the more he emancipates himself from necessity, the less important he feels.

—W. H. Auden

There is no doubt that in America we define ourselves by our work, even by our job titles. What, then, happens to our identity when we retire? Surely, this need to adjust or re-create our self-image is among the most crucial of the psychological, emotional, and spiritual needs of retirement.

How we cope with the issue of self-image has much to do with our individual make-up, as well as the degree to which we identified with our job, our degree of satisfaction with the job, and our needs for recognition and reassurance. When he retired from a college teaching career, Carl Klaus noted ruefully:

Now that I'm retired, I shouldn't care what the world thinks of me. . . . Retirement, it seems, doesn't really free one from the hungers of a lifetime, for the need for some kind of affirmation and recognition. . . . I had grieved over the end of my teaching career, in part at least because I regretted the loss of affirmation that comes from a life in the classroom.[1]

Sociologist and gerontologist Joel Savishinsky defines this identification with work as a peculiarly American trait that is not shared by the rest of the world. He quotes Stefan Nokalsky, a retired hotel executive:

See, I'm a Depression baby, a product of "you got your job." I try to fight that idea, but it's how I am. It's so American. Europeans don't begin conversations by asking "What do you do?" But here, what you do *is* who you are. . . . Otherwise, it's "Who are you?" Your answer: "Stefan Nokalsky!" They think, "What's a Stefan Nokalsky?"[2]

Nokalsky linked work with character, with a satisfaction that comes from within:

Success is in the mind, not someone else or your job telling you you've made it. . . . I have this guilt problem, the need to set goals and do useful things. . . . So much of me—too much—is the Protestant ethic or *Poor Richard's Almanac:* self-development, purposeful hobbies.[3]

The retirees in my own survey grappled honestly with the issue of self-image and resolved it in a variety of ways. For one woman, a very successful financial advisor, the solution was a new self-definition:

During the first year, I felt I had lost my "title." Now I feel I have a new profession via board work, networks, travel, new skills.

And a female advertising executive pinpointed the problem even more specifically, referring to some gender differences:

This is the biggest issue related to retirement! You feel you've lost your identity when you no longer have a title after your name. I think this is even a bigger issue for men vs. women. Most professional women I know seemed to have transitioned into retirement more quickly than the men I know. In fact many men who retire have actually gone back to some form of business.

One dissatisfied early retiree, Bob, was formerly an executive with a large company (we will hear more from him later). Bob candidly admits:

[I felt a] terrible sense of loss at retirement, because so much of my self-image was tied up in my job. I was manager of large organizations for the majority of my career and my accomplishments resulted from the work of other people. When the people and the secretary and the corner office went away overnight, I started to see myself as a useless old man at age fifty-five.

However, he continues:

In my current life I no longer feel that loss, even though I still don't have the organization or the corner office or the secretary. I have a greater appreciation for the importance of my family and friends, and I find that all I really need as a "replacement" for work is intellectual stimulation, daily association with people, and a sense of purpose.

(How Bob resolved his dilemma so well will be one of the subjects of chapter 11.)

Meanwhile, many retired men and women solve the identity and self-image problem in more traditional ways. A prominent communications executive states that she gets self-worth through active volunteer work. Another retired advertising executive states, "I've certainly questioned my self-image, but fundamentally have grown in my own eyes as I've tackled new things." For one woman who entered the work force in her forties, after her children were grown, the issue of self-worth was hauntingly familiar and perhaps more easily solved:

> As I had a period earlier (twenty years) when I did not "work," my retirement feels more like that stage. My wish for my self-worth image is to continue to make a positive difference in the lives of others.

Retirement is a stripping away of our former self-definition. As our retirees testify, it is an opportunity to discover who we really are. When one door to self-definition is closed, we look for other doors, other paths, other dreams. But retirement is a transition, and loss is at the core of every transition. We give up an image of ourselves, and this is not an easy task. One woman, Lois, admits:

> Before I made the decision [to retire], I struggled with these things. My self-worth, I know, is tied to my creativity. If I use that in writing, art, gardening—I will be very satisfied.

She solved the self-image problem her own way, before retirement, by combining her interests and avocation in volunteer work.

Thus, the first challenge of retirement is to discover "*Who* am I?" instead of "*What* am I?" And it is crucial that we meet this challenge. If we are unable to redefine ourselves in retirement, two unfortunate consequences may follow. First, we may view ourselves by externals only, by how we appear to others and how many toys and trappings we have accumulated. For most thoughtful people, this failure to leave the past behind is a shallow substitute, and it fails to supply enough meaning for our new phase. The second consequence is that we may find ourselves stuck and unable to move on with our lives.

Suicide statistics provide a sobering confirmation of the importance of a new self-definition for retirees. The highest suicide rate for all age brackets is found among Caucasian men aged 72 and older.[4] A telling example is George Eastman, founder of Eastman-Kodak Company, who ended his life just two months after retirement, leaving a plaintive note: "My work is done, why wait?"[5]

Our American culture tends to socialize males to a singular focus on work-as-identity. Early in life men learn that their purpose is to work, and all too often their success in life is measured strictly by the yardstick of how successful they are as workers. Women, at least until recently, received a different message from society. They were supposed to work outside the home but only temporarily, until they settled down and had children. Work was always supposed to be secondary in their lives, taking a graceful back seat to their "natural role" as nurturer, wife, and mother of a family. When retirement comes, therefore, women often find it easier to step back into a caregiving role, which supports them psychologically. (This gender difference may, of course, diminish or even disappear for the generations of young women who are now defining themselves more by their work roles.)

In our society, work and age influence both the roles we take on willingly and the roles that are assigned to us. (As John Lennon once said, "Work is life, you know.") These twin factors so largely shape our identity that when we stop working, we confront our own (and society's) stereotyping of age.

In a youth-obsessed culture, age itself seems to be the enemy. (If you doubt this, just scan some so-called humorous birthday cards aimed at people in their mid-thirties and beyond.) Thanks to the aging of the baby-boomer generation, this trend is changing, but for now, the double whammy of retirement and growing older brings changes in how we view ourselves and how others view us.

As shown by the retirees in my survey, the experience of retirement involves not simply age but *perception* of age. The self-perception of retirees centers on many things, including their own expectations of what they should have achieved by now, their relationships with others, how others see them, and often a sense that time is slipping away.

Perhaps this is a good place to differentiate among the concepts of self-image, personal identity, and self-esteem. Self-image has a great deal to do with the value you place on yourself, whereas personal identity revolves around the role (or roles) you play. One has to do with your value to yourself, and the other relates to your value to others. Together, they contribute to your sense of self-esteem. Your adjustment to retirement will be easier if you can separate your personal identity from your role as a worker.

Typically, if you have a high degree of self-esteem, a strong self-image, and a fairly well-defined sense of personal identity before retirement, they will not dissolve when you retire. It's worth noting that transitional experiences (including the transition of retirement itself) can strengthen self-image, boost self-esteem, and even solidify personal identity. Listen to the voices of retirees in my survey who did just that. A retired dentist said:

> My self-image was always high and I never needed the support of others to keep it propped up. I accomplished all of my goals as a dentist and quit at the top. Being active in my community and condo helps build my self-worth.

Or the words of a retired teacher:

> Yes, my self-image has changed since I retired from teaching. I am no longer a "teacher." But I don't feel guilty or apologetic about this. I did something noteworthy, I made a difference in the lives of many (not all) of my students. I worked successfully with staff and this is a wonderful feeling. I know that my children were proud of the fact that I went to work full time in my forties but they began to think I was never going to leave the classroom. . . . But self-worth comes from within, and for now, things are intact! I feel good about who I am and what I am.

For some retirees, their level of self-worth remains stable in retirement. One woman entrepreneur told me, "I don't think my self-image has changed. I am proud of the success I had in business, but it was time to move on." She adds, ruefully, "I do find it hard to recognize that Council of Aging issues apply to me!"

A physician in the process of retirement, agrees:

> I used to think this [self-esteem] was an issue but really don't anymore. When you get to this age, you have stopped defining yourself by your work; that's a younger person's mindset. In listening to my retired friends, some of whom were potent leadership types, this issue almost never comes up. When it does, it's often a comment about poor Charlie, who can't let go.

For some retirees, retirement even offers an opportunity to improve
or enhance their self-image. A retired architect, now active in his club,
declares:

> I think my self-image has improved, because at age 60 I was able to put
> myself in a position where I could do what I wanted to do when I wanted
> to do it. I never dreamed that I'd be in that kind of position at age 60,
> and I even impressed myself.

He continues, thoughtfully:

> I also think that being president of a prestigious club and being able to
> effect significant improvements to that organization has filled the need
> for continued personal success. I've used my management experience to
> turn the club into a sound business operation, and I've used my marketing
> background to improve the level of communication throughout the or-
> ganization. These tasks are no different from what I did in my professional
> career, I just don't get paid for my time anymore. . . . They're good for
> the ego, but they also result in a lot of job satisfaction, which in turn
> makes you try even harder.

Another retired executive agrees:

> Avocational interests were well developed in advance of retirement. I
> believe my self-image has remained the same because of the kind of vol-
> unteer activities (financial, historical, civic) I pursue.

A retired neurosurgeon declares:

> Today, I think of retirement as reaching a stage in life when you can
> round out your image regarding some of the things that you couldn't find
> time to do in a career limited by the tyranny of success and the desire to
> be the best in your vocation.

And so we seem to have come full circle. For some, retirement signals
the beginning of a downward spiral of self-esteem and self-worth. For
others, whose self-esteem was high before retirement, it remains at the
same level, thanks to their own ability to add desired roles or activities.
And for other lucky individuals, retirement brings the welcome opportunity to expand their life possibilities, take on new roles, and greatly
enhance their own self-image and sense of self-worth by adopting a new
(and perhaps more desired) identity. Moreover, they seem to seek out
like-minded people. As one retired executive points out,

[self-esteem is] not a problem. . . . so many of the people we now meet are in the same boat. They have less to prove. Maybe those still driven don't retire.

Clearly, these latter two categories of retirees developed a healthy self-image *before* they retired and had the personal strength to maintain it in retirement. For those just in the planning stages of retirement, there are significators of a healthy self-image. The first step is to assess your own self-image and its degree of health. Some questions to consider include the following:[6]

1. How do you feel about yourself now, and why?
2. Has your self-esteem changed since retirement (if you have already retired)? If so, how?
3. Rate how positive your self-image is, based on a scale of 1 ("I see myself as really ineffective") to 5 ("I see myself as really effective")?
4. Explain your answer. Why do you feel this way?
5. Rate the clarify of your sense of personal identity, based on a scale of 1 ("I'm confused and uncertain about my roles") to 5 ("I'm clear and certain about my roles").
6. How much of your self-concept is affected by the way others see you?
7. What diminishes your self-image and what strengthens it? What do you need to sustain a healthy self-image?
8. If you need to, how can you begin to build a positive self-image?

The second step in building a healthy self-image in retirement is to come to terms with the concepts of aging and youthfulness. For most of us, retirement is synonymous with aging and therefore has an unpleasant connotation. We ascribe certain negative attitudes and behaviors to an advanced age and project those attitudes and behaviors onto ourselves and others, regardless of their appropriateness. What is even more confusing is that we often mistakenly pronounce the developmental tasks of youth as good while the tasks of later years seem unpleasant or unfortunate. While few of us relish the idea of growing old, fewer of us long for its alternative! Since aging is a natural and inevitable stage of life, what attitude should we adopt toward aging?

Why is it that some 40-year-olds seem ancient, while other people well beyond 90 display the lighthearted, bright attitude that we associate with youth? (Think of the late Queen Mother of England, who apparently retained her youthful, fun-loving spirit until her death at 101.)

What qualities (beyond chronological age) contribute to the feeling and perception of youth? Let us consider the essence of youthfulness, in the spiritual if not the physical sense.

Youthfulness is irrelevant to age. It is an intense involvement with the process of life that helps us thrive at any age. In fact, we could say that being chronologically young paradoxically can hinder the development of youthfulness, since one must be very mature to express this quality. It is an attitude of vitality, freshness, curiosity, and honesty that gives color and variety to one's existence. There are ways to enhance youthfulness, especially as we approach retirement:

1. Change your attitude about aging. Aging is the necessary means for transforming our lives. Instead of viewing aging as a thief, stealing all that is dear to us, think of it as a master teacher. Rather than seeing aging as the end of a journey, see it as the beginning.

2. Try to resolve old conflicts and grudges. Forgiveness is ultimately liberating.

3. Give something back. Service enhances the energy of life and connects us to the world and other people.

4. Develop a grateful heart. Avoid blaming and criticizing behavior.

5. Learn to laugh at yourself. Build a sense of humor that can transcend the aches, pains, and tears of aging and help you embrace life with vigor.

6. Continue to grow, learn, and investigate new things. A youthful zest comes from sustaining an interest in things outside ourselves.

7. Engage in a healthy lifestyle, balancing exercise, rest, and nutrition, to slow the aging process.

And consider the dryly humorous advice of one of my survey respondents:

8. "Keep moving and shave every day."

We have all met people who have been retired for years but still continue to define themselves by their former profession or job title: "I'm a retired doctor," "I'm a retired sales manager." This response is understandable but unfortunate. The key question to answer (and be comfortable with) is, who are you *now?*

In order to answer that question satisfactorily and honestly, you need to first ask yourself what additional roles or activities in society are (or could be) important to you *now?*

American society is often criticized in the world community because we have no specific societal roles for retirees. However, this may be a blessing rather than a curse. Since no roles are prescribed, you have an abundance of choices. You can choose or create the role you want in retirement. For example, you might want to review and reconsider some or all of the roles and identity possibilities open to you described in chapter 4.

Retirement allows us to do many things, including looking closely at ourselves. In some ways, the great challenge of retirement is to listen profoundly to the life lessons that aging offers and to appreciate its new curriculum. Gratitude is the most powerful antidote to aging and poor self-image. To make the most of the aging process, we can adopt attitudes of profound thankfulness for all that has gone before, a recognition of our own giftedness, and an appreciation that everything (including aging and retirement) are our best teachers. These attitudes help us to remain open to the life that lies ahead.

Points to Remember

- Self-image is critical to the retirement process.
- Successful retirement requires an ability to redefine yourself and develop a sense of purpose.
- Changing your attitudes toward aging and separating yourself from your roles is important in adapting to the retirement phase.
- The challenges of retirement, well met, can boost your self-esteem.

NOTES

1. Carl Klaus, *Taking Retirement*, 31.
2. Joel S. Savishinsky, *Breaking the Watch*, 124.
3. Ibid., 125.
4. Richard P. Johnson, *Creating a Successful Retirement*, 7.
5. Ibid.
6. These questions are adapted from an evaluation scale presented by Richard P. Johnson in *Creating a Successful Retirement*, 120–22.

6

—⟨∞⟩—

It Takes Two: For Better or Worse—But Not for Lunch?

A busy man's retirement needs to be coordinated with his (probably) busy wife's schedule.

—Survey respondent

Grow old along with me! The best is yet to be,
The last of life, for which the first was made.

—Robert Browning

The words of poet Robert Browning capture the spirit with which most married couples enter retirement, with visions of "the best is yet to be"— blissful time together enjoying the good life. For many retirees, that poetic aspiration does epitomize their experience of retirement. (However, Browning's own wife, Elizabeth Barrett Browning, died before him and he was unable to experience those idyllic later years with his beloved spouse.)

The impact of retirement on marriage is profound. In many ways, it is similar to the effect that retirement has on self-image and self-esteem. A marriage can either be enhanced or greatly challenged by retirement. Recent surveys by major corporations showed that the second largest group of employees seeking divorces was among those who had recently retired and had been married for 30 to 35 years.[1] Not surprisingly, a critical predictor of the success of a partnership in retirement is how well the partners got along before they retired, in terms of communication, tolerance, respect, and commitment to the marriage. As you might expect, the requirements for a successful postretirement marriage include honesty, empathy, and a willingness to be flexible in adapting to the changing rhythms of marital life.

Indeed, while retirement offers another chance to redefine marriage, take on new roles, and explore new horizons (either together or separately), retirement can also create a whole new set of problems. Since most retirees have been married for at least 20 or 30 years, patterns, responsibilities, and boundaries (regarding finances, household duties, and social life) have become set and may be difficult to change. Even the "turf" of the marriage, the home, may become part of the problem, since for a while, at least, both partners will share the same turf, perhaps for the first time in their lives.

The first thing to note about the demographics of couples in retirement is that they seem to fall into three categories: (1) couples in which both spouses work and both retire (Track A), (2) marriages in which both spouses work and only one (usually, but not always, the wife) retires (Track B), and (3) marriages in which one spouse (usually the woman) did not work and the other spouse retires (Track C). In each of these tracks, the impact of retirement can be dramatically different, and in each case, the rewards and challenges also differ.

In Track A, in which both spouses work and both retire simultaneously (or the second spouse retires soon after the first), there is great potential for a wonderful adjustment. But the potential also exists for a bit of tension. Without the stresses and routines of work, both partners must motivate themselves to fill the empty time and the social vacuum created by the loss of challenges and relationships formerly found at work. Most of our survey respondents on Track A, however, reported either no significant changes or an improvement in the marriage after retirement:

> "Retirement has improved my marriage because I'm less stressed. I have enjoyed making new friends, appropriate for a new lifestyle and new interests."

> "No difference in marriage."

> "Marriage is better: less stress, more comfort. Things get done for both of us."

> "I now have friends (which I never had time for before). In fact, I don't know how I had a career and a life, in retrospect."

In Track B marriages, in which only one spouse retires while the other keeps on working, the challenges are different. There may be potential conflicts in time management and role expectations. However, almost all of the survey respondents in this category reported a high level of satisfaction in marriages where one spouse retired. One respondent replied,

> My husband is very pleased to see me return to being laid back and casual. I'm trying to rekindle friendships that got put on the back burner for years. I can see my children and grandchildren without feeling I am carved up in little pieces.

Track C marriages, in which one partner (usually the husband) retires and the other has not worked, may force unexpected challenges. For example, one retired executive in my survey states:

> So far, our marriage is holding up just fine, although I must say we've had to adjust to an increased level of togetherness. The most interesting aspect is that there are no weekends and sometimes you have to check the calendar to see what day it is. . . . In retirement you have more time to spend on things other than your business career, which for most of us was at least 80 percent of our daily activity.

Typically, the "nonworking" wife, by this time usually finished with child-raising responsibilities, may have developed new interests of her own—a hobby, serious volunteer commitments and board positions, or even a new career. Now that her spouse is free, he may want to take off and travel just at the point when she prefers to stay home and reap some of the rewards of her local networks, volunteering, or part-time employment commitments. How can she balance these enjoyable new activities with the expectations of her newly retired husband? Either way, the couple no longer has the diversions of work or children. They are really free (or forced) to focus on each other, and now their relationship is in the spotlight in a whole new way. The survey respondents from Track C dealt honestly with the strains of balancing the new demands on couples at different places in their lives. One retired man admitted:

> My wife was not ready for my retirement. I just said, "Let's go." She always had obligations to hold her back. So she had to resign many posts. By then I did not want to "go" as much.

You can hear in his voice the stress involved in the seesaw situation, in which each partner discovers different needs and values at retirement and shortly thereafter. It's almost as if this newly retired man and his busy wife pass each other like ships in the night. As one is ready to take off, the other values commitments and a life close to home.

Another retired executive (who, following his early retirement, has returned to work) remembers that earlier dislocation and speculates on the future:

> My retirement was a special problem for me because my wife was working and I found myself home alone more than I wanted to be. Now that we are both working again, things have returned to "normal." For our next act, I expect to be working for a period of time when she is retired. I wonder how that will work out, but she says she is looking forward to some time by herself following a busy career.

Still another retired executive wisely notes:

> The effort that is required to make a successful marriage work involves different sensitivities, as the circumstances of existence after retirement are different. It is not "business as usual," as the usual has been altered by the state of retirement.

Retirement is a time for significant decision-making around such issues as money, travel, use of leisure time, and (perhaps) moving, and all of these choices require the active collaboration of both partners, plus negotiation, honesty, empathy, accommodation, and compromise. Old, unresolved issues may surface, and outside interests and new relationships may prompt feelings of jealousy. Moreover, hobbies that replace time formerly spent together may threaten the relationship or at least cause some stress.

At the very least, both partners need to sharpen their communication and conflict-management skills. Never before has open, honest, and respectful communication been more important than at this stage of the marriage. Because few couples leave work at exactly the same time, the event of one partner's retirement is likely to affect the quality of the relationship.

There are also significant gender differences in how couples view retirement. Men are more likely, for example, to have difficulty leaving their work and career identities behind, whereas women are much more likely to experience social (and sometimes financial) vulnerability when they retire.[2] These days, many women's careers are just hitting full stride as their husbands' careers wind down. The fact that his wife is now the breadwinner (and still valued in the marketplace) can be devastating to some men. A retirement researcher advises any man likely to retire to make early preparations for an interesting postretirement life, so he won't mind that his wife is still working.[3] Women who have invested much of their time and efforts in maintaining friendships and family ties find that it pays off in emotional and social support from those relationships when they retire; whereas men, traditionally less likely to have built up a network of relationships, may be particularly vulnerable in retirement or if their spouse divorces them or passes away.

Why do women typically fare better than men in retirement? One reason may be that they have learned (perhaps the hard way) to keep busy outside and beyond the workplace. Call it the "housewife's revenge," but it does seem that for many women, after their own retirement, their many activities provide them with more than enough to do, with basic homemaking responsibilities plus time spent with children, grandchildren, and friends, they feel there is reason and purpose for getting out of bed every day.

What advice do the experts on retirement have for couples as they begin their retirement? The advice the best experts give revolves around the importance of communication. (This was also echoed by my survey respondents.) At this time of life, communication may become more important than it was earlier in the relationship. Some of the experts' suggestions for improved communication are given below:

- Find ways to honestly, but tactfully, share your feelings and ideas.
- Share your problems and your daily lives, even the trivial details that make up a shared life.
- Ask what you can do for each other. Also ask for what you need.
- Avoid hurting each other or belittling each other's activities.
- Try to boost each other's self-esteem.
- Avoid letting one spouse control the agenda and the marriage.
- Work to maintain intimacy as a source of great nourishment.[4]

This new state should prompt a reexamination by both partners of the primary issues of retirement. Where do you begin this reassessment? Consider your need for privacy in your normal work environment. Do you have and cherish your own desk, cubicle, office, or suite—a space that's yours alone? When you retire, you give up that space. What do you have at home to replace it?

In moving home, many retirees tend to expand their areas of influence and take over the whole house, as if it were theirs exclusively. (A classic example is the husband who takes over the kitchen, reorganizing it and changing everything his wife had done.) Both husband and wife have a need for private physical space. (Nonworking spouses need their own space too and need to speak up in order to protect it.)

Ask yourself, what area in the home is available just for me? Determine a space that can be allotted to you; perhaps an area or a room can be converted into a den, computer room, home office, wood workshop, library, or art studio.

Aside from physical space, ask yourself if you (and your spouse) need some private "mental space." You each need to do some activities alone without accounting for each moment of your time.

Also, try to remember why you married each other in the first place. In the hectic first few years of marriage, it seemed that you never had enough time to spend together. Well, here's your chance in retirement. Rediscover each other, but remember that having a splendid relationship doesn't mean that you must spend 100 percent of your time together. Each of you is an individual, so give each other the time and space you need to be a complete person. The more whole you are as an individual, the more you have to share with your partner in retirement. In retirement, think of the marital relationship as a new merger, not a takeover!

There is an old saying among soldiers that "combat makes good men better and bad men worse." The same might be said for retired couples. A bad marriage probably won't improve if couples have more time together, but a good marriage probably will get better.

After all, a marriage really is a *series* of marriages, not a static entity. Just as the early honeymoon years differ from the child-raising years, so will the retirement years differ from the career-building years. Couples will need to make their own rules and adjust as they go along. In fact, a good marriage is constantly being reshaped and redefined by the partners as they respond to the needs and pressures of each new stage in life, including retirement. As one of my respondents wisely observed about marriages in retirement:

This may be true for some couples with good marriages. They can weather illness, loss of friends, family, etcetera, but I would agree that more couples fall into the less-than-perfect category.

One change that occurs as one grows older is that life takes on a bittersweet quality—friends, family die, days are precious, life moves faster— one becomes less apt to overreact to small problems (even large ones) and approach life more philosophically.

The couple piece is important, I know, but one can only be a good partner when one is comfortable with oneself.

Couples who have invested the time and effort over the years to build a strong relationship, who have honed their communication skills, and who view themselves as a team and not as competitors may find the retirement years the best years of their married life—"the last . . . for which the first was made," in Browning's words.

Finally this sage advice from Dr. Joseph Drake of Davidson College is worth remembering:

> Enter retirement with a good wife (or husband), a good family, a good home in a good community, good health, a good income, a lot of good luck and a good attitude. Do what you want to do when you want to. Don't worry about dying, it happens to the best of us—except old soldiers. And finally, keep the hell out from under your spouse's feet.[5]

Points to Remember

- The impact of retirement on marriage, which can be both positive and negative, is always profound.
- Couples' reactions to retirement depend somewhat on the "tracks" they are on.
- Retirement issues require good communication skills and joint adjustments by couples.
- There are significant gender differences in the way couples view and adjust to retirement.
- Good marriages respond to the needs and pressures of each new stage in life. A good marriage can find retirement to be the best stage of all.

NOTES

1. Cited in Phil Rich, Dorothy Sampson, and Dale Fetherling, *The Healing Journey Through Retirement*, 157.

2. Joel S. Savishinsky, *Breaking the Watch*, 242.

3. Ralph Warner, *Get a Life*, 144.

4. These and other suggestions are found in Phil Rich, Dorothy Sampson, and Dale Fetherling, *The Healing Journey Through Retirement*, 173–74.

5. Quoted in Eben Alexander Jr. M.D., "The 'Retired' Chairman Syndrome," 19.

7

—∝∞∝—

For Women Only: The
Pioneering Generation Retires

> Retirement may be looked upon as either a prolonged holiday or as
> a rejection, a being thrown onto the scrap heap.
> —Simone de Beauvoir

Perhaps the most significant development in the workplace in the last
quarter of the twentieth century (rivaled only by the emergence of the
computer) is the increasing presence of women at the management and
executive levels. In unprecedented numbers and with unimagined consequences, women entered the doors of corporate America and even rose
to the highest levels. Not surprisingly, then, when these women retire,
they will create a new, dynamic factor in the demographics of retirees.
Never before have so many high-powered women executives retired.
How will this group of powerful retired women act? How will their
retirements be different from men's retirements? The retired career
woman is a recent phenomenon because "career woman" itself is a relatively new idea.

One of my respondents reminds us how far working women have
come:

> I had no picture of retirement whatsoever at age 25. Career expectations
> were different for women in 1966. By way of illustration: At the midpoint
> of my freshman year in college, I approached the head of the political
> science department for career advice. Although he had chosen me to be
> a part of a 10-student honors seminar, he could not imagine that *as a
> woman* there would be much to do with a major in political science. It
> isn't surprising that I expected I would work only until I had children.

What are professional women's special issues? Do they have greater or lesser difficulty with retirement than men? Is self-image a problem?

Once again, let's turn to the respondents in my retirement survey. There was a small number of women executives in my sample. For most of them, retirement represents a relief—a gift of time and a chance to pursue other interests.

> "Thirty-four years is enough! My husband was retired and I decided to join him."

> "I see it as a chance to see whatever became of the other side of me that I had to abandon in my pursuit of a serious career."

> "Work was no longer providing the satisfaction and stimulation to keep me motivated."

> "I felt that I had accomplished all I set out to do when I started my career; now I wanted to see what else was out there for me."

Only one or two admitted that they retired because they saw they "had gone as far as they could" in the corporate environment and felt they could accomplish no more. Although most admitted that self-image and self-esteem were issues, they felt they had resolved these issues nicely:

> "I get self-worth through active volunteer work."

> "At first it was a problem. I missed having a secretary and a title! But I soon got over it as I became immersed in my new life—travel and volunteering."

> "I have a new satisfaction in life without the financial (and other) stress."

> "I still feel very good about myself."

> "I feel fortunate in where life has taken me and curious and hopeful about where else it may lead."

The women I surveyed most often cited travel, exercise, and extensive volunteering as their areas of preferred activity. However, even these outlets prompted some reflection and concern on the part of the women executives.

> Volunteer work and committees are wonderful. . . . but remember that many of these activities have been started and run by women who have never worked, or who have not worked since marriage. Their ideas of time management, how to run a meeting, etcetera may be a rude awakening to those of us trained to work efficiently and completely on-task.

They will have a different notion of time and flexibility, and often hold meetings for social as well as task-oriented reasons.

There may be more rude awakenings and culture clashes as high-powered women ease into retirement and begin to make their own volunteer contributions to the community. And their number is dramatically increasing. A recent article in the *New York Times* by Alex Kuczynski, "They Conquered, They Left," featured a group of executive-level women who voluntarily chose retirement. The article profiles high-level, soon-to-be retirees such as Oprah Winfrey; Rosie O'Donnell; Governor Jane Swift of Massachusetts; Candice Olson of iVillage; Carol Wallace, managing editor of *People* magazine; and Cokie Roberts of ABC television. (Of course, it is only fair to note that Ms. Winfrey has recently reconsidered and decided to recommit to her talk show for several more years and Ms. O'Donnell discontinued her talk show career in order to pursue other interests.) However, all these women plan to relinquish positions of power and fame well before the traditional age of retirement. Why would they abandon the high rung of the ladder when they are so powerful?[1]

Several answers are offered by executive women. The most intriguing (if unproved) theory is that women have a different psychic investment in their careers than men do. Dr. Phyllis Moen, a sociologist at Cornell University who has studied gender differences in the workplace, claims that it is easier for women in powerful jobs to quit all at once rather than to scale back or work part-time.

> You're seeing this now because the way careers are structured, women in high-status jobs can't reduce it, so they have to quit cold turkey. Imagine being a part-time governor. You can't do it.[2]

However, women at all levels have often retired early, usually for lifestyle (family) reasons. Unlike men, who seem more reluctant to give up their work, women seem more willing to leave work voluntarily (when they can afford it) and explore other areas of life. Some theorists (and some women executives) claim that men form long-lasting identities with their corporations or institutions. Carol Wallace, the retiring editor of *People* (who plans to settle in a remote Scottish village) states:

> Men never leave jobs. Men die or get forced out. They are addicted to the power and the status and the games. . . . But they're missing something. . . . I don't want to drop dead in my job. I want to be ambulatory.

But maybe their DNA says they'd drop dead if they didn't work, that it's their oxygen. But it's not for me.[3]

Geraldine Laybourne, founder of Oxygen Media and former president of cable television for Walt Disney Company and ABC, admits, "I don't know if it [giving up all the corporate perks] would have been as easy to do if I were a man."[4]

However, according to Sheila Wellington, president of the business women's advocacy group Catalyst, the picture drawn by these high-profile women retirees is skewed simply by their small numbers. "There are so few women at the top," she says in the Kuczynski article, "that each singular drop-out takes on a heightened and unrealistic significance."[5]

It cannot be denied that women at the very top seem more prone to dropping out than men do. Perhaps this is because they can afford to. In a Harvard study of 902 women who graduated from its professional schools between 1971 and 1981, 25 percent of the women who earned Harvard MBAs in the 1970s had left the workplace entirely by the early 1990s, despite their expensive training. Perhaps that partially explains why Rosie O'Donnell and others have considered leaving the rigors of a demanding media career: if you *can* quit, why not do so? But for most women, the answer is more complex. Certain circumstances (financial freedom, family support) give women the freedom to retire, and the equal freedom to admit it. "I want a life," said Cokie Roberts when she retired from television.

But clearly there is more to this male-female difference in early retirement, because many financially successful men can also afford to retire. One theory suggests that women take their jobs and responsibilities more seriously than men and tend to burn out quicker. Another possibility is that some women who reach the top look around and ask themselves, in the words of the old Peggy Lee song, "Is that all there is?" They decide it's not worth the stress, and so they choose to leave.

In an interview published in the *New York Times Sunday Magazine* of June 23, 2002, former advertising executive Mary Wells Lawrence speculates that most women lead "horizontal" rather than "vertical" lives— that is, because they tend to be involved in doing a variety of things (being horizontal), including their jobs, relatively few of them rise to the top. Only a few women (the vertical ones) choose to focus on their jobs and rise to the top of their professions. Retirement offers an opportunity for these high-powered women to change their focus and add the horizontal dimension to their lives.

Perhaps that is what differentiates women from men. Women are able to separate their work from their identity, and to recognize more that there is a rich life beyond work. As one recently retired woman executive in my survey comments:

> I think it is easier for women to retire because they have been acculturated to develop networks that allow social supports, feel that work is not the only way to give, have typically learned to balance home, family, work, friends, etc.

Carl Klaus muses on the different responses of men and women on retirement when he contrasts a colleague's reaction to her own retirement to his own angst:

> But Barbara didn't say much about her career as a social worker or about retirement, even when I questioned her closely about it, which made me notice again how differently men and women have been acculturated to think about working and retirement. Or so it seems they were in the past, in my generation and earlier.[6]

He goes on to speculate as to whether this cultural difference is a current phenomenon that will change with the next generations of women workers:

> Nowadays, with women employed in the full range of jobs and professions available to men, I wonder if women's attitudes toward retirement will be so different from those of men, so comparatively subdued. . . . I wonder how my younger women colleagues will respond to retirement when they start approaching it some ten or twenty years from now.[7]

My survey respondents echo these gender differences in their ability to separate their identities and self-worth from their high-powered work identities. As one woman, a retired senior vice-president of a bank, asserted:

> So far this [self-image] hasn't been an issue for me. I am very involved with community work, but also do not feel overly tied to my former title.

It bears repeating here what one of my respondents said in chapter 5, about the issue of work as identity:

> I think this is even a bigger issue for men versus women. Most professional women I know seem to have transitioned into retirement more quickly

than the men I know. In fact, many men who retire have actually gone back to some type of business.

Another woman executive said:

> I have been very fortunate for two reasons: I have worked all my adult life from desire rather than necessity; my husband has been very supportive and interested in my work. I have also been fortunate in having two distinct careers.

Another important issue for women executives is the lack of role models, especially in retirement. More than one of my female respondents commented on this subject. Here is a typical response:

> My generation of women did not usually work outside of the home. But this was not because they weren't able and educated to do so; rather it was the cultural mode of the time. However, these very able women had dual roles. They were orchestrating life at home, but they were and are the major volunteers in highly responsible positions. . . . They gave of time, expertise, energy, and yes, money. I admire this investment of self. However, in terms of retiring from full-time professional employment, I have seen more men, usually physicians but not exclusively so, involve themselves in all sorts of volunteer work.

There are sure to be more female role models in retirement as more of the pioneer group of women executives retire and decide where to focus their time and energy.

WOMEN AND THE GUILT-EDGED RETIREMENT

Guilt is another issue peculiar to women retirees and mentioned by several of my respondents. As one early retired executive put it,

> So much effort and expense, not to mention careful mentoring, was put into my career that I almost felt guilty at retiring. I had a sense of letting people down.

A retiring physician, aged 50, echoes this sentiment when she says, "Particularly in the competitive world of medicine, it seems almost wasteful and disloyal to quit." And a retired religious administrator and teacher admits:

> I think I still have a twinge of guilt about not earning but I believe I now
> have a *better* appreciation of my gifts and talents.

Often, women feel that they are letting other women down by voluntarily leaving the field, because their training was so expensive and their
admission to the higher ranks of business and the professions (especially
law and medicine) has been so recent. As one woman admitted, she
feels as if she is giving ammunition to those in our society who say that
advanced training and promotion are "wasted" on women since they
will "just quit" anyway. According to Sheila Wellington, the president
of Catalyst, an organization that supports working women, each retirement symbolizes all women because there are so few women at high
levels retiring, and so the retiring woman feels that her career must
represent and legitimize all working women's career aspirations.[8] Her
voluntary abandonment of a career (especially if she is younger than the
traditional retirement age) is thus seen as a disappointment to women,
particularly to aspiring, younger career women.

For the retired career woman who has worked hard to demonstrate
her commitment to her job and to overcome obstacles to her own rise
and promotion, a sudden return to the home can, and often does, affect
her self-esteem. Previously seen as competent and professional, she now
is seen as "just a housewife" by many people and may have to nurture
her own sense of identity and self-esteem in order to counteract the
stigma of society. Of course she can overcome this stigma; she is, after
all, the same person. But the issue of self-esteem remains for many
women.

SINGLE WOMEN RETIRING

A special category of retired female executives has another major issue
to deal with. This is the group of women who are single, either through
lifelong choice, divorce, or widowhood. Their number is increasing, not
only because many marriages end in divorce long before either spouse
is ready to retire but also because larger numbers of working women
have chosen to remain single and devote themselves to a career. What
are the special issues for these single women in retirement?

Paradoxically, being single is both an advantage and a disadvantage.
The newly retired career woman does not have to fall back on stereo-
typical housewife and caretaker roles. She is free to create a retirement
designed to her own satisfaction, with no (or few) outside and family

responsibilities. She has also probably prepared well financially for her retirement and can live where and how she pleases.

Yet there is a downside to singleness. If this woman has found fulfillment, responsibility, and identity in her work, she may suddenly find herself in a life that seems without direction and support. Although she developed a healthy self-esteem that certainly served her well in a career and will serve her equally well in retirement, she also may face society's changed view of her. In society's eyes, she has "fallen" in status from being a successful career woman to being merely a woman who never married or had kids. This is not the case, however, for divorcees or single mothers. For a single retired woman, finding her niche in retirement can be as great a challenge as finding her niche in the executive suite. The divorced or widowed retired woman may have an easier time, as she presumably can rely on a larger family structure (children, stepchildren, grandchildren, in-laws, etc.), but she will still face the same problems as any other retired woman in developing *new* relationships in retirement.

However, for the time being these issues are problematic for only a relatively small number of retired women. Even the single retired women in my survey reflected the confidence and self-assurance that enabled them to have high-powered careers and will serve them equally well in retirement. One speaks for many as she said, "I've certainly questioned my self-image but fundamentally have grown in my own eyes as I have tackled new things in retirement."

The beauty in all of these responses is, of course, the concept of *choice*. Not long ago, women were made to feel incomplete without a mate and were not even considered able to train for and sustain high-powered, challenging careers. Thanks to the changes brought over the last 30 years by the women's movement and an increased interest in women's psychology and issues, there are more options of every kind for women today. Perhaps the next frontier for these newly retiring, pioneer-generation feminists is to explore and redefine the very notion of retirement.

Points to Remember

- Women have special issues in retirement, although they generally adjust better than men do.
- Travel, exercise, and volunteering are the preferred activities of retired women professionals.
- Women can more easily separate work from identity and value the "horizontal" as well as the "vertical" in life.

- Guilt may be a factor that women professionals must deal with as they retire.
- Single, divorced, or widowed women retirees each have significant retirement issues, especially in replacing the social network provided by work.

NOTES

1. Alex Kuczynski, "They Conquered, They Left," *New York Times*, 24 March 2002, 7–8.
2. Quoted in ibid., 7.
3. Quoted in ibid., 7.
4. Quoted in ibid., 7.
5. Quoted in ibid., 7.
6. Carl H. Klaus, *Taking Retirement*, 21.
7. Ibid.
8. Quoted in Kuczynski, 8.

8

———— ✥ ————

With a Little Help from My Friends: Resources for Retirement

> The key questions change every decade or two in life. You wonder at 10: Is there life after death? At 20: Is there work after college? At 40: Is there sex after marriage? At 60: Is there life after work?
> —Joel Savishinsky

As you set out on your journey of retirement, you will soon find that you don't have to navigate alone. Many experts are available to help you—role models, financial planners, health care professionals, and organizations that cater specifically to older adults and retirees. Moreover, you will also find specialists in education, travel, and the spiritual life, as well as (and perhaps most important) friends and family members ready to help. Let's look more closely at some of these resources.

VALUES CLARIFICATION: THREE EXERCISES TO HELP WITH PLANNING

You are your own most valuable resource. As you begin planning your retirement, trust your own heart, mind, and soul. What do you now feel drawn to? What is important to you right now? Where and how do you wish to spend your precious time? The following Values Clarification Exercise will help you clarify your thoughts and set the stage for your retirement planning.[1]

Exercise 1

Directions: In the spaces below, on the left, identify things (i.e., events, relationships, activities, etc.) that you are *moving away from* as you approach (or live out) retirement. In the spaces on the right, identify what you are *moving toward.* (For example, you might be *moving away from* "group activities" and *moving toward* "solo activities.")

As I approach my retirement, I am (or will be) moving:

Away from . . .	Toward . . .
1.	1.
2.	2.
3.	3.
4.	4.
5.	5.

Exercise 2: Skills and Dreams

1. At this stage of my life, what skills do I want to *learn?*

2. What skills do I want to *use?*

3. What have I always wished I had time to *do?*

Exercise 3: Your Personal Mission Statement

Write your own personal mission statement. It can (and should) be succinct. It should capture the purpose you now envision for your life. Examples of personal mission statements might include:

"I plan to use my management and organizational skills in my volunteer work in the community and to learn new skills, specifically in computer technology and art history."

"I see my mission as devoting myself to family and friends and creating a happy network of sustaining relationships."

Now write your own mission statement:

It is important to understand that your personal mission statement is flexible and that you can change it as your understanding of your purpose in retirement develops.

After you have completed these three exercises, you are ready to embark on the next stage of planning. Now it is time to learn what kind of help is available for you. Who are your retirement guides? Who can you ask for help?

MENTORS AND ROLE MODELS

The first person to search for is a good mentor or role model. This can be someone famous whose use of retirement you admire, but it can also be someone closer to home, preferably someone you actually know. When asked if they had any role models for retirement, that is, someone they admired or who was doing what they aspired to, the retirees I surveyed gave diverse replies:

"I admire people who work for others."

"No one in particular . . . I envied all retirees who seemed to be happy, while I still had to work."

"I admire the people who have found balance. I think there is a decided lack of role models. My father died before age 50, and my mother worked until her late seventies."

"My parents used their retirement to help others. My mother taught adults to read. My father did Red Cross work. They stayed active in the community and with their grandchildren."

"I have always admired Jimmy Carter and his work with Habitat for Humanity."

"I admired the 50-year-old friend who moved to Santa Fe and rides horses every day. I admired my retired engineering friend who finally took up his passion for art. I admire another friend who wrote a book. And people who volunteer to help. I admire anyone who is happy with what they are doing."

"I admire those who . . . involve themselves in all sorts of volunteer work. . . . They take their talent and use it in admirable and instructive ways."

"My parents are my role models . . . and my grandmother who got an M.A. in 1894!! Quite a woman!!"

"[Someone who] does volunteer work, travels, and is a master gardener, a new skill."

Yet, perhaps significantly, others did not point to any one role model for retirement.

"I know lots of retired people whom I admire, but I'm not sure I'd consider any of them retirement role models. Everyone is different and everyone has different objectives."

"My retirement was not patterned on any one individual, although I did garner ideas from many friends. Fortunately my activities evolved naturally from others who know my interests."

In the first category, Jimmy Carter is an example of a person who has made admirable use of a forced early retirement. Although he was only 56 years old when he lost the election in 1980 and left the White House, he refused to be limited by the term "former President." Ironically, he has achieved some of his greatest success since leaving office and turning his energies to the larger world. He founded the Carter Center, through which he has organized several humanitarian projects (including monitoring elections) and sponsored health programs in Third World countries. He inspires volunteerism by his hands-on work building houses for Habitat for Humanity, he has written 16 books, and in 2002 he received the Nobel Peace Prize. In his so-called retirement, President Carter has achieved a stature and respect he never experienced during the peak of his power as president!

Famous people like Jimmy Carter, while inspirational, are seldom personally available to answer your questions about retirement. For personal and immediate answers, you need someone closer to home, someone more readily accessible. If you know where to look for them, you can find numerous inspiring retirees who have made the most of their roles in the last third of their lives.

As one woman retiree in my survey explained,

I didn't use any resources nor was I aware of any. I did observe the choices people made and how they seemed to work out. It's certainly a topic of discussion among our peers, but usually from the male point of view, assuming that the wife will adapt.

She goes on to say:

The best resource I have found *since* retiring is a book *The Last Gift of Time* by Carolyn Heilbrun.[2] It addresses living a fuller life and aging.

Another woman describes her retirement role model as

My former neighbor and dear friend. . . . She retired several years after her husband. . . . She knew when she was ready to move on to a different phase in her life and she has successfully blended meaningful community work, continuing education, spirituality, travel, and close contact with her far-flung adult children.

One begins well before retirement by nurturing friendships and developing warm and trusting relationships (which may be unrelated to work). Seek them out in your extended family and in the network of contacts you have built up over the years. Surely you can find someone who has made a successful transition to retirement.

When you find someone who you think could be an interesting mentor or role model, arrange to meet with him or her. (You'll know you've found the right mentor if he or she is so busy that it's hard to make an appointment.) Don't be afraid to ask the tough questions about loneliness, boredom, security, and loss. Ask this prospective mentor how he or she has dealt with such issues. Successful retirees are usually resourceful and eager to share their insights with you. Since they have overcome some of the things you fear, you can be sure they will help you to see the positive side of your own retirement. As one retired woman in my survey discovered, with the inspiration of a mentor or role model, you can craft your own positive future:

My parents' example of retirement seems more and more valid to me each year: keep interested in things, apply yourself, keep busy. Be mentally active and curious.

For some of you, as for some of my survey respondents, no mentor or role model may be necessary. For many self-directed souls, a lifetime of observation, especially of family and friends, provides enough inspiration. Following are comments by some of the retirees I surveyed:

> "My retirement was not patterned on any one individual, although I did gather ideas from many friends. Fortunately, my activities evolved naturally from others knowing my interests."

> "I know lots of retired people whom I admire, but I'm not sure I'd consider any other retirement role models. Everyone is different and everyone has different objectives."

> "I now have many friends who are fully retired and I have learned from parts of their stories. As everyone is different, no model fits all."

Most of my respondents have constructed their own successful retirement models out of parts of other lives that they have observed. And one woman confidently said that her model is

> "Myself! I love not working. But it helps to have a passion, something you love and can indulge."

MAINTAINING YOUR HEALTH

As important as finding a role model is maintaining your health for the rest of your life. The better our health and physical fitness after age 55, the better our retirement years are likely to be. Most adults are now aware that they can influence and control their own health by eliminating smoking, eating a healthy diet, exercising moderately, controlling blood pressure and cholesterol, managing stress, and getting necessary medical tests. Research has long confirmed the strong link between nutrition and health. We can, to a large degree, control and influence our health by paying attention to what we take inside us. Quite literally, we are what we eat. The following are the basic dietary guidelines for Americans published by the U.S. Department of Agriculture and the U.S. Department of Health and Human Services:

- Eat a well-balanced diet.
- Maintain healthy weight.
- Choose a diet that's low in fat, saturated fat, and cholesterol. It's recommended that 30 percent or less of your calories per day come from fat.
- Choose a diet with plenty of vegetables, fruit, and grain products.
- Use salt in moderation.
- If you drink alcoholic beverages, do so in moderation.

We now know that lifestyle is a crucial factor in sickness and health, especially in old age, when the effects of a lifetime of habits, good or bad, become obvious. The causes of many illnesses are found in our environment, lifestyle, and emotional balance. In fact, some of the most important determinants of a healthy older age are the very rules that we've heard over a lifetime, and the prescriptions for clean living echo the guidelines just given:

- No smoking

- Moderate drinking

- Seven or eight hours of sleep a night

- Regular meals with no snacks in between

- Breakfast every day

- Normal weight

- Moderate and regular exercise

Since they can do so much to improve our life, it seems obvious that nutrition and a healthy lifestyle are crucial to a successful retiree. In addition to taking good care of yourself, it is useful to read some of the excellent monthly magazines or newsletters that may keep you motivated to stay healthy.

Other health practices helpful to retirees are those we all know we should maintain throughout our lives, although we seldom take them seriously enough. During the retirement years, these needs assume greater importance. *Managing stress* is a highly individual task; one man's (or woman's) high stress is merely another's necessary stimulation. In general, if you keep your weight down, eat well, and exercise every day, a moderate amount of stress should not pose a problem. However, increased drinking and eating, poor sleep, and chronic depression are signs of stress that need to be addressed.

Getting *necessary medical tests* (including an annual physical checkup) is a powerful tool to maintain health, since spotting and correcting problems early increases the chances of a healthy and happy retirement.

The last and most significant health resource is maintaining the *habit of exercise*. The key to sticking with an exercise regimen is to find an exercise you enjoy. If you enjoy it, you are more likely to keep doing it. Swimming, jogging, jazzercise, fast walking, bicycling, aerobics, mall walking, and kickboxing are all terrific workouts as long as you have access to them on a regular basis

As recently as 30 years ago, experts believed that conditioning after 40 had little effect and even that exercise after 60 produced no dramatic improvement in fitness and functioning. However, in 1967, Dr. Herbert de Vries, professor of exercise science at the University of Southern California, tested those notions. He discovered that healthy older people who engaged in appropriate exercise benefited just as much as younger people. In fact, more recent studies have shown that men and women in their eighties can still increase their muscle mass and continue to grow stronger. Frail older people can benefit from specially designed strength and resistance training. In fact, with strength training programs, a selected group of nursing-home residents (averaging age 87) under the direction of Dr. Miriam Nelson of Cambridge, Massachusetts, increased their walking speed and ability to climb stairs. Some were even able to discard their walkers in favor of canes instead. Competent and skilled athletes continue to perform well up through age 65. And professional athletes who continue to train can remain active in their seventies, eighties, and even nineties.[3]

We now know that exercise is valuable at any age, but it's possibly more important the older you get. Ironically, just when we think we're becoming too old to exercise and plan to give it up, exercise becomes critical to a successful and healthy older adulthood!

Different exercises have different purposes. For example, stretching promotes flexibility, range-of-motion exercise helps maintain a joint's complete movement, strength exercises help muscles contract and grow stronger to do more work, and endurance or aerobic exercise can improve the body's ability to use oxygen.

The overall effects of exercise are dramatic and proven. Exercise can decrease body fat, improve circulation, and lower your blood pressure. It improves endurance, adds strength, produces flexibility, and continues to build muscle—all highly desirable results. Some studies have indicated that exercise wards off certain kinds of depression by helping the body produce endorphins, the natural mood elevator. (Not surprisingly, the ability of exercise to combat depression and anxiety is increased if the individual exercises with someone else. Since as many as 25 percent of people over 65 suffer from depression, this potential habit of exercising becomes even more significant for older Americans.) Finding time to exercise is a challenge at any stage of life, but the increase in leisure time during retirement should make it easier to develop and continue the habit of exercise.

Since we all know by now that exercise is good for us, why don't we engage in it on a regular basis? The issue is not lack of information (we've been bombarded with health information for years), but rather the obstacles that prevent us from exercising, eating well, and maintaining a healthy lifestyle. Here are some typical reasons (or excuses) that 6,000 preretirees gave for not doing what they knew they should:

- I have no time to exercise.
- I feel fine and look good. Why change?
- This information is not relative to my life.
- Rich food tastes great.
- I'm exhausted at the end of the day. The last thing I want to do is exercise.
- It's hard to break a habit and change.
- My husband (or wife) isn't very supportive of change.
- I'll have more time in retirement for this healthy behavior business.[4]

Let's hope that last statement at least is true. In the meantime, what is your favorite excuse? Resolve to overcome it—and lead a healthier, happier life in retirement. The message is: you are in charge of maintaining your health and it's never too late.

YOUR FAMILY LIFE

Nurturing and maintaining good family relationships (and mending those that are broken) is another important step for ensuring a happy retirement. As you age, the psychological (and practical) need to feel part of a supportive family will grow. Unfortunately, this can happen just at the same time as your ability to create or maintain family ties declines. Given the length of life after retirement, you can see why the positive effects of a loving family structure are so important in a retiree's life.

However, as in every other relationship in life, the relationship with family members requires maintenance and constant nurturing. If we expect family members to be there for each other, to love and care for each other, we have to nourish those relationships and invest time and effort to keep the ties that bind. You need to develop balance, so that you are not dependent upon your children and they are able to live independently while you maintain a mutual attitude of respect, admiration, and caring. Some practical (and perhaps obvious) tips to help you build or maintain good relationships with your family include the following:

1. Spend more time with your children.

2. Keep up your relationships (through phone calls and e-mail if necessary) with parents, siblings, nieces and nephews, grandchildren, and cousins.

3. Consider carefully before you decide to move far away from family members.

4. Be inclusive in your definition of family. Those who are generous in defining family in early life and midlife enjoy richer retirement relationships.

5. Be willing to take on the role of family leadership if needed. (Sometimes a vacuum of leadership develops due to the death or relocation of a previous leader.)

6. Consider having periodic reunions or newsletters for extended family members.

7. Try to develop a sense of humor about lifestyle differences.

8. Don't give up on dropouts or black sheep. Stay in touch and keep the doors open.

9. Get quick and effective help if a family member has physical or psychological problems.

10. Don't let divorce ruin a family. Try to remain neutral and include all parties at gatherings, if possible.

The best advice in maintaining a strong family unit is to cultivate a spirit of tolerance and acceptance. Making the effort pays off in dividends for the rest of your life.

YOUR SOCIAL NETWORK

In many ways, our friends nurture and define us better than family can. For one thing, friendship is voluntary. No one *has* to be your friend in the way that others *have* to be members of your family. Moreover, our friends share some significant part of us—our past, our interests, our current or past roles, our values. Often our friends understand and value us more than our family does. Staying close to friends can therefore provide for a rich and happy retirement life. A fascinating 1998 University of Michigan study reported that the most powerful predictor of life satisfaction after retirement was the size of a person's social network.

Those who expressed their satisfaction with life averaged social networks composed of 16 people, whereas those who were less satisfied averaged networks of fewer than 10 people.[5] But the reverse is also true: people who are isolated and lonely are more likely to become ill and die prematurely.

Generally speaking, we have two kinds of friendships: interest-related and deep. An interest-related friendship happens as a result of common interests among friends, such as a similar hobby or a club. A deep friendship involves a more intimate relationship that transcends shared interests. It usually creates an unshakable bond.

Ironically, the number of friendships is likely to decline just when you need them the most. Older people generally have smaller social networks than younger people, and those networks contain a larger number of family members than do those of younger people. And yet, older people in general appear to find higher satisfaction in their relationships with friends than with family members. (This is probably because many people live across the country from their blood relatives and have created their own families out of close friendships; this is especially true of retirement communities.)

Here, too, we find important gender differences. Older women tend to have more friends than older men do, and they are likely to place greater value on their friendships. Older women seem more likely (and able) to share activities and emotional involvement than men. For older married couples, the wife is likely to have a friend as her closest confidant, while the husband's confidant is likely to be the wife. For both sexes, however, friendships remain valuable in retirement.

It is a truism, alas, that friends change, and old friends move away or die. You have to constantly replenish your friendship circle by making new (and younger) friends. A wonderful book called *The Art of Friendship* discusses the importance of friendship in modern American life:

> When family ties falter, when love affairs or marriages end, friends relieve our loneliness, fulfill our need for affection and bolster our morale. Making and keeping friends may be among the most important things you can do for yourself. . . . Remain open to establishing new friendships, which allow you to start with a clean slate . . . to concentrate on the process of "creating yourself."[6]

Here are some suggestions to help nurture and increase friendships:

Make some younger friends.

Seriously commit yourself to continuing to make new friendships in midlife.

If you are married, make some friends who are yours alone.

Plan to live around enough compatible people later in life so that you'll have the opportunity and incentive to form new friendships.

Form new friendships around common interests and shared values.

Be committed to your friends. Take your responsibility to maintain and nurture your friendships as seriously as you take your obligations to your family.

When possible, recover old friendships. These are often the most meaningful touchstones in life. Invest time and energy in staying connected. Attend those reunions!

Join groups that promote or focus on your hobbies, sports, or intellectual pursuits.

Volunteer with a group working for a cause you believe in.

Become active in a church or other spiritual group.

EDUCATIONAL RESOURCES

Educational resources may turn out to be the retiree's best friend. Now that you have enough time, you can enrich yourself by learning a new skill, developing a new intellectual interest, or pursuing a long-deferred college degree. You can even choose to share your own valuable knowledge with others. There are generous educational offerings through universities, colleges, community colleges, and distance-learning centers.

Nearly 500 universities now offer exciting opportunities for lifelong learning in special programs for retirees. The institutions vary markedly in size, mission, and curriculum. Some have fewer than a hundred student members, while others have more than a thousand. There are small private colleges, large public universities, and community colleges; they may offer four-week classes, single lectures, or full semester courses. The colleges may be travel-oriented, while others are rigorously academic. For example, Harvard University's Institute for Living in Retirement has, for the past 25 years, offered continued educational growth to 500 members annually. Harvard's size permits students and graduates to maintain a spirit of collegiality, and the curriculum is an academic buffet designed to appeal to a wide range of intellectual interests and tastes—from Buckminster Fuller to Zoroastrianism, and from W.E.B. DuBois to the Supreme Court in the twenty-first century. Because the Institute's faculty members are among the best in the fields of medicine, engineering, law, business, government service, and the arts, Harvard does not need to hire additional professional faculty to run the courses. In addition to attending lectures, membership in the Institute requires active participation in at least one study group each semester. According to the peer learning concept, Institute members create, coordinate, and participate in study groups, taking responsibility for sharing their knowledge and experience with each other. Because of the need to maintain a cap of 500 on the membership, only a limited number of new members can be admitted each year. The Harvard Institute, like many other retirement educational programs, seeks candidates who are intellectually committed to group study, lively discussion, and oral reports and who show a willingness to serve on one of the program committees.[7]

Similarly, Brandeis University (in Waltham, Massachusetts) offers an Adult Learning Institute that comprises a broad range of directed study groups on a variety of subjects, with 5 to 20 participants who meet for 10-week semesters. The emphasis within this noncredit program is on peer leadership and participation, which are sustained by an atmosphere of sociability and mutual encouragement. Although most of the study groups are led by peers, many are conducted by former professors and visiting specialists.[8]

Lest you think that only northeastern universities offers such programs for retirees, I will mention 2 more of 300 hundred national programs. Duke University in North Carolina has its own Duke Institute for Learning in Retirement (DILR).[9] DILR is a community of adults over 50 who participate in a liberal arts curriculum. The instructors are a mix of peer teachers, Duke professors, graduate students, independent scholars, and community experts. There are no tests, grades, or educational requirements, but participation is essential—from contributing to class discussion to sharing the results of one's own research. DILR describes this kind of learning as "all carrots and no sticks."

And, in the Deep South, the home magnet for many retirees is the University of Miami at Coral Gables, Florida, which offers the Institute for Retired Professionals. The programs at the Institute provide an "outlet for the creative use of the experiences and talents of the retired person within the cultural environment of the university." Everyone is welcome. The only prerequisite is a desire to continue learning in a relaxed atmosphere. Once again, the core of the Institute's program is the courses and study groups that are created and led by the members themselves, constituting a "university within a university" and including a variety of disciplines.[10] In the West, similar programs are offered through the University of California's statewide campuses as well the University of New Mexico, to name only two examples.

Educational opportunities for retirees are not, of course, limited to the United States. Oxford University and the University of Edinburgh are two exciting examples of foreign study opportunities. Oxford University offers a Lifelong Learning Program through the Department of Continuing Education with participation in the famous Oxford tutorial programs.[11]

The University of Edinburgh's Office of Lifelong Learning provides courses lasting from a half-day to two years in a wide variety of courses. There are no entrance requirements or formal examinations.[12]

A further intriguing innovation in education for retirees is the creative solution of Lasell College in Newton, Massachusetts. According to the June 10, 2002 issue of *Newsweek*, Lasell College has established a retirement facility on the college campus, with a requirement that elderly residents ("Lasell Villagers") attend a full course-load of classes until a doctor certifies that they can no longer attend. Lasell's idea of turning retirees into perpetual undergraduates has caught the interest of gerontologists and retirement-home operators, who are trying to adapt the program around the country.[13] Before moving into the facility, each Lasell Villager must agree in writing to complete a full course-load every year as long as health permits. Two hundred highly accomplished retirees now live and study at tiny Lasell. Instead of tuition, Villagers buy their apartments (which cost from $180,000 to $650,000) and pay monthly fees for meals, healthcare, nursing-home insurance, and instruction. A kind of Leisure World with course work! Encouraged by medical research suggesting mental fitness may ward off dementia, retirees are spending less time on golf courses and more time in halls of learning.

Similarly, Institutes for Learning in Retirement, located at various campuses across the country, also sets up classes for the elderly. Nearly 70 colleges and universities, including the University of Virginia, Ithaca College, and Oberlin College, have opened retirement facilities and about 25 more are in the planning stages.

For a more casual approach to learning, you might consider Elderhostel. More than 800 colleges and universities all over the world offer educational programs to adults who are over 60. These courses last one week and are conducted by highly trained faculty from the universities sponsoring the program, offered at reasonable rates. All facilities are provided for Elderhostelers, including room and board, field trips, and educational supplies. Programs are also available overseas in Europe, South America, Australia, and even China. The overseas courses last three weeks and of course include extra transportation costs.

One of the most intriguing Elderhostel programs is "The Experience at Oxford," located at Britain's oldest university. Elderhostel offers a rare opportunity to share in university life, for members can stay in the historic university residence hall and attend lectures and take field trips to the city center, famous museums, and a Royal Shakespeare Company performance, as well as excursions to Stratford-upon-Avon, the Cotswolds, and Dorchester. The 14-day program is a typical, if very intriguing, offering of the Elderhostel program.[14]

In addition, many cities offer "university retirement" courses through local universities. Organizations such as the Union Institute in Cincinnati, Ohio and the Fielding Institute in California offer distance-learning degree programs.[15]

You can also pursue your education without any structure at all. There is a constantly growing supply of books on tape and videotapes released by prominent universities and institutions like the National Geographic Society and the American Management Association. The AARP offers wonderful educational texts through the Scott Foresman Publishing Company.

Retirees can also give back to the community, as many agencies and institutions can make use of their skills to provide counseling and conduct seminars in business subjects such as financial planning, communication, supervision, and sales management. SCORE (Senior Corps of Retired Executives) provides advice and expertise to new businesses through chambers of commerce or small business associations. The International Business Executive Association even offers opportunities for retired business leaders to share their knowledge on overseas assignments! There are also wonderful opportunities for tutoring, volunteering in inner city schools or acting as a mentor to young people.

As you can see, there is no limit to the possibilities for gaining and sharing knowledge in retirement. Having witnessed more change than any generation in history, retirees represent a wealth of untapped knowledge, wisdom, and valuable experience. You can share much-needed insights and perspective with a new generation.

TRAVEL

For many people, travel is the best part of retirement. Not only does it offer a change of scene, a breath of fresh air, and a new perspective, but it also serves as a divider between work and retirement. It helps us change pace. In that sense, travel can be a defining event for the retiree.

Because of discounts, frequent flyer programs, and the ability to travel at off-peak times, many seniors (especially those adventurous enough to bypass luxury hotels) find they can cover lots of foreign ground at a relatively modest cost. Elderhostel, for example, sponsors reasonably priced educational travel programs that include knowledgeable guides and lecturers. By working with a "house trade broker," it's even possible to arrange to spend a month or more living abroad with little or no expense for lodging. The Internet is a fruitful tool for finding travel opportunities or bargains.

Travel can be the ultimate time extender, the best reenergizer. It's a guaranteed departure from the norm and an entrance to the fresh and new. As poet Yehuda Amichai, tells us, "Travels are the soul / of this world. Travels remain forever."

When we travel to unknown places, we can be free to reinvent ourselves, even if this reinvention is only temporary, or we can act as young as we feel. Since nobody knows—or cares—who we are, we are free to do or be whatever calls to us. Travel makes life new, fresh, and stimulating again. Probably because we are free of our "old" self and learning new things in a new environment, we feel more alive, more alert, more open while traveling. Travel in the post–9/11 world is not easy or stress free, but the freedom and intensity of experience it offers is priceless.

For the extremely adventurous and physically fit, there are highly specialized trips revolving around adventures (African safaris, whitewater rafting, extreme skiing, or mountaineering) or projects (an archaeological dig, for example). Whatever your pleasure or your pocketbook, travel offers stimulation, purpose, and enrichment to retired people.

Points to Remember

- Values clarification and definition of personal mission are the most important first steps.
- Take advantage of all the help and resources available in retirement (role models, family, friends, financial planners, health resources, education, travel, and Internet resources).
- If you are not already computer literate, retirement is a good time to learn to use a computer and take advantage of its many benefits.

NOTES

1. Based on an exercise developed by Richard P. Johnson, *Creating a Successful Retirement*, 137.
2. The Heilbrun book is listed in the Bibliography.
3. Steven Shagrin, ed., *Facts about Retiring in the United States*, 89.

4. Ibid., 91.

5. Cited by Ralph Warner in *Get a Life*, 112.

6. Quoted in ibid., 113. The book is Ernest Callenbach and Christine Lee-feldt, *The Art of Friendship* (New York: Pantheon Books, 1979).

7. For information, contact the Harvard Institute of Learning in Retirement, 51 Beattle Street, Cambridge, MA 02138; phone (617) 495-4072. The website is www.hilr.harvard.edu or you can email sheehan@hudce.harvard.edu.

8. The Brandeis Adult Learning Institute can be reached at (781) 736-2171 or at its Web site: www.brandeis.edu/bali.

9. You can contact DILR at (919) 684-2703 or www.learnmore.duke.edu/DILR.

10. For information phone (305) 284-5072 or visit the Web site at www.education.miami.edu/irp.

11. For information, consult the Web site at www.ox.ac.uk and www.conted.ox.ac.uk or telephone +44 (0) 1865-270000.

12. To contact the OLL, call +44 (0) 131-650-4400 or e-mail at oll@ed.ac.uk. The Web site is www.lifelong.ed.ac.uk/about/contact/html.

13. Peg Tyre, "R is for Retirement," *Newsweek*, 10 June 2002, 48.

14. To obtain more information, contact: Elderhostel, 80 Boylston Street, Suite 400, Boston, MA 02116, tel. (877) 426-8056 or visit www.elderhostel.org.

15. The Union Institute can be reached at (513) 861-6400, www.tui.edu; and the Fielding Institute is at (800) 340-1099, www.fielding.edu.

9

───◈◈◈───

Why Do You Want to Retire, Anyway?: The Uses and Misuses of Retirement

When people are too concerned with how they "occupy" their leisure, their free time takes on a rather unleisurely character.
                                                        —Josef Pieper

Before we launch any further into the dos and don'ts of successful retirement, it seems appropriate to pause here to consider our *purpose* for retiring. In many ways, our answers to the questions "Why did you retire?" or "Why are you planning to retire?" will determine the success or failure of our retirement.

In chapter 1, I noted that there is, obviously, a vast difference between voluntary retirees, those who *choose* to retire, and those who have retirement thrust upon them. Those who choose retirement do so for clear and beneficial reasons. Presumably, if they follow through on their intentions, they will feel happy and fulfilled. As for the others—those who are forced or persuaded to retire—they will presumably have a much harder time enjoying or making a success of their retirement.

Well, perhaps the above statements are only *partly true*. To begin with, if voluntary retirees have not clarified their own attitudes and purposes (or if that is not realistic or achievable for them), they will remain unsatisfied no matter how often they assure others (and themselves) that they are thrilled with their retirement. Conversely, those who were led or pushed into retirement can decide, *once they have accepted the inevitable*, to create purpose from their retirement and then set out to fulfill it.

Some of the respondents in my survey did just that. Bob, a retired executive of a large company who was asked to step aside for younger managers, found his remaining options with the company unattractive:

> I obviously saw that coming and had every intention of doing just that [taking the new job offered]. However, at the last minute, while on vacation in Alaska, it came to me that it would be a mistake for me to end my career doing something that I really didn't want to do. I have never regretted that decision.

As we will see in chapter 11, Bob went on to reinvent himself and design an extremely satisfactory retirement for himself.

Thus, once you have recognized and accepted your options, it is important to seek clarity of purpose. What are the appropriate uses of retirement? My respondents found ways to rejuvenate, revitalize, and even re-create themselves on their life paths. A retired surgeon found the opportunity to "change offices" instead of retiring and to "take on new challenges that round out my image or permit expression of creativity related to my long-range goals." Another retiree found "an opportunity to develop sides of myself I did not have time for while working and to learn new skills." One retired business owner confessed that "it's wonderful to be in control, answerable and responsible only for myself, accountable only to my loved ones." Another woman was very clear about the purpose and timing of her retirement: "My retirement was by choice and was precipitated by my sixtieth birthday, that seemed a proper milestone of sorts, and most importantly by the birth of my first grandchild. I wanted my time to be more flexible."

Regardless of whether your retirement was chosen or not, your first step is to become crystal clear about the *purpose* of your retirement, even if you have to invent or adopt a purpose after the fact. Ask yourself these four simple (though perhaps not easily answered) questions. (It may be helpful to record your responses in a journal.)

1. Why *exactly* did I retire?
2. Regardless of why I retired, do I now see my retirement as an opportunity? For what purpose?
3. Is there anything that I've always wanted to do that I can do now? What specifically might that be?
4. How would I now like to *use* my retirement?

Your honest and thoughtful answers to these four basic questions are likely to help you find the purpose of your retirement.

Retirement is not a static, one-time event. It is a life stage, a process. We will continue to change, even in retirement, and we will continue to grow. For this reason our purpose will also grow and change as our retirement life (and life itself) grows and changes. As many of my respondents learned, during the first "honeymoon," or vacation, stage of retirement, we are often led to new purposes, so we must be flexible and open to change. One retiree explained it this way:

> The first year was wonderful. I went to Ireland to play golf for twelve days. I went to Florida to play golf for two weeks. I went to Virginia to play golf on four different occasions. And I played golf at my own club three or four times a week. I began my writing career and I was elected president of my club. [But] after two years, I am starting to look for other types of endeavors in the area of golf facilities consulting, where I can use my architectural, business, and club-management experience. I also have an opportunity to become involved in a brand-new golf publication . . . in addition to my writing.

Another retiree discovered that she had not stopped growing:

> I found the first year of retirement very difficult after the first burst of energy—at last I could organize all those photographs, attend to those neglected closets, read a book in one sitting, etcetera. When I had done as much of that as I would ever do, it was time for a reassessment. . . . I then thought of things that would give me pleasure and some new skills. I took a computer course at the library and also at the local community college. I took bridge lessons at a nearby community center and an Italian conversational course at a local community college. I successfully ran for an elected office. I feel that I am "on track" and content with my level of activity.

Her retirement is a work in progress, and she seems pleased with the way it is developing. She is also aware of the need for constant reassessment of her purpose in retirement.

In his wonderful book, *The Spirit of Retirement*, James A. Autry suggests several tips to help you begin the transition to retirement, which can even help those who are already retired:

> If most of your work life has been spent with other people, practice being alone. Get comfortable with your own company. (Please note that being alone does not include television watching or surfing the Internet.)
>
> If your job has involved working alone, do the opposite. Learn to be with other people. Volunteer in some group activity.

Do something different—particularly if this activity involves something you might like to do in retirement.

If you've been involved in an office setting, juggling words and numbers, begin working with your hands. Build something, garden, or start a craft.

If your job has been physical, use your free time to put your mind to work. You may choose to read, attend plays or concerts, or take an adult education course.

You might want to get some psychological counseling (just as you obtained financial counseling) to deal with your transition to retirement, particularly if it has been especially stressful.

Have discussions with your spouse and/or partner about your mutual expectations of retirement.[1]

As we refine and rediscover our purpose, some further questions to ask ourselves are:

1. What would you like to accomplish in the years ahead?
2. What's really important to you? If you knew you had six months to live, how would you use them?
3. Are you living the life you want to live?
4. What's missing the most from your life right now?
5. What do you need to do to prepare for what lies ahead?

These five questions are, of course, basic life-planning questions that anyone should ask at *any* stage in their life or career. They assume a special and poignant significance for retirees trying to define (or create) a purpose for their later stage of life. This, in fact, is the profound function of retirement.

Now let us look at the downside. What happens without planning? When we do not plan our lives, often we misuse an opportunity that life gives us. Retirement without planning often leads to squandering of the chance of retirement and results in sadness, boredom, or frustration. Each of these misuses (or perhaps abuses) of retirement will be discussed separately, including poor planning, boredom, sudden uprooting and relocation, and the failure to meet our own needs.

We discussed poor planning in chapter 2. Even though a few of the successful retirees in my survey insisted that planning was unnecessary and, in some cases, unrealistic or even counterproductive, for most of them, planning was essential in creating a meaningful life in retirement.

As one respondent told me, "I really feel that I was able to hit the ground running in my retirement because I had thought so much about it ahead of time and knew exactly what I wanted to do with it and how I would use my time. I couldn't wait to begin!"

But enough said about planning. There are those whose temperaments don't require it (or who actively resist it). For the rest of us, though, planning seems to be important if we want to make the most of our retirement.

The second misuse of retirement, boredom, is a very familiar fear to those contemplating retirement. "But what will I do all day?" is a common cry, not only of the workaholic but of all those who recognize the significance of purpose in our lives. Boredom is a legitimate fear, but it can be overcome by planning and by careful attention to deciding on the purpose of your retirement and fulfillment of that purpose. (You may recall the process of structuring discussed in chapter 4.) A statement by an unhappy retired man quoted in *The Psychology of Retirement* underlines the dangers of boredom:

Once you retire, you simply must find some kind of rewarding activity or you are sunk. There is a definite retirement vacuum, a state of dull, witless and pointless idleness. I can speak for no one but myself, but I wish to God I was back on the job.[2]

The third misuse of retirement is sudden uprooting or relocation without thought, plan, or purpose, yielding loneliness and alienation from life. As we saw earlier, the decision to move—whether from a large home to a small apartment, or across the country or world—is a deeply significant one, fraught with unintended consequences. Unless you know exactly *why* you are moving, and unless you have carefully thought out the consequences of that move (the losses as well as the gains), you may be risking the lonely feelings that come from being cut off from the environment and people who help sustain your life.

The fourth potential misuse, failing to meet your needs, is significant. As stated earlier, work itself satisfies five basic human needs: financial security, time management, sense of purpose or usefulness, status, and socialization. A successful retirement must fulfill many of these needs. Answer the question "Why am I retiring?" with a statement that articulates a clear purpose, and you will have gone far to satisfy at least three of the human needs that your previous work satisfied: time, status, and socialization.

Some of the successful retirees in my survey were very careful to continue to meet the needs previously satisfied by their preretirement work. A retired female executive in her fifties described her deliberate and purposeful planning for satisfaction: "The first year [of retirement] I networked—made connections with people who were on boards in which I was interested. Now I'm *too* busy—need to cut back on a couple of things!"

A retired banker gave the following advice:

It's always nice to be thought of, so perhaps I accepted too many consulting and other interesting opportunities immediately following retirement. These opportunities absorbed more time than I had planned, so I suggest others might be more selective in the early months.

Neither of these two retirees needed to worry about boredom, poor planning, or failing to meet their need for greater purpose. Even though they describe themselves as overcommitted in retirement, their satisfaction and delight shine through in their answers.

In fact, each of the successful retirees surveyed had three positive qualities in common. First, they had well-developed retirement plans and purposes. They did not make abrupt or unsought changes; they knew what they wanted to do and how to follow through.

Second, they created and maintained very positive attitudes toward retirement. They were full of optimism and embraced the challenges ahead.

Finally, the truly satisfied retirees possessed a clear and accurate picture of retirement. They were well aware of the issues surrounding retirement and had done enough planning to ensure that these issues would not be stumbling blocks. Instead of misusing the great gift of time that is retirement, they took advantage of their own (self-chosen or not) opportunity to revitalize and recreate their own lives in retirement. In finding or defining for themselves a *purpose* in their retirement they made it a success.

Points to Remember

- Know *why* you want to retire. If you've been forced into retirement, design your own reason or purpose.
- Ask yourself how you would like to *use* your retirement.

- Planning ahead can reduce or eliminate the abuses of retirement—lack of meaning, boredom, uprootedness, and failure to meet your own needs.
- Attitude matters!

NOTES

1. James A. Autry, *The Spirit of Retirement*, 32–33.
2. The Everyday Psychologist, *The Psychology of Retirement*, 28.

10

❦

Retirement Is Not for Sissies: Avoiding the Black Holes

Life inflicts the same setbacks and tragedies on the optimist as on the pessimist, but the optimist weathers them better.
—Martin Seligman

Now that we have looked at the uses and misuses of retirement and what you might expect, especially during the first year of retirement, let's look at the downside. How can you avoid some of the pitfalls of retirement?

First, the good news. Researchers who study life satisfaction in retirees conclude that those who are satisfied with their lives before retirement will probably also be satisfied in retirement, because they have learned to adjust to life's vicissitudes. ("Life satisfaction" is a term that encompasses zest for living, taking responsibility for our actions, inner resolution between desired and accomplished goals, a good self-concept, general happiness, optimism, and spontaneity.)[1]

But the opposite is also true. If your life satisfaction is low while you are still working, your self-esteem and overall satisfaction will not change dramatically after your retirement. Retirement planners used to believe that if people were happy in their work, they would not want to risk unhappiness by retiring but would prefer to keep on working. Now, as research proves otherwise, we can say that current life satisfaction becomes both a yardstick and a predictor of future happiness in retirement. A satisfied person is generally happy and optimistic, relishes life, and has a strong self-concept.

Symptoms of low satisfaction, on the other hand, include apathy, a sense of uselessness, and pessimism. Of course, we all know retirees who exhibit these negative traits, and we probably wish to avoid them. So how do we prevent the black holes of depression, alienation, loss of purpose, loneliness, boredom, and isolation?

Once again, there is good news. As psychologists and spiritual writers have been telling us for years, happiness is an "inside job." We are the authors of our present happiness, which in turn predicts our future happiness in retirement. It is not the job by itself that creates our happiness (or lack of it), but what the job represents. As we learned in chapter 2, in retirement we need to replace the five benefits of work: (1) financial security, (2) time management, (3) sense of usefulness or purpose, (4) status, and (5) social contact or socialization. We also need to measure our current (and therefore future) satisfaction in six crucial areas of life. To get you started, try assessing your own life satisfaction.

1. My work life _____
2. Family relationships _____
3. Relationships with others _____
4. My overall self-esteem _____
5. Spirituality _____
6. Leisure (what I do when I don't have anything else to do) _____

(As a reality check, if you are married, you might also ask your spouse to rate the same areas of life satisfaction. Then it is helpful to discuss the results.) Try assessing your own satisfaction in these areas right now in the blank following each term. This will give you a simple profile of the degree of contentment you feel right now. Happiness arises in us as a result of our own internal appraisal of how well life is going right now.

Another predictor of success in retirement is finding the right reason to retire. Many preretirees spend years longing for their retirement. They just can't wait to retire. But when they are asked why they want to retire, they have no clear plans—they just want out of their current jobs. Their reason for retiring is thus negative, not positive.

Consider the case of Marilyn, the manager of a large retail store who has full responsibility for the total operation. Marilyn did a good job; while not absolutely thrilled with her position, she had mastered it and was reasonably satisfied with it. She was not, however, satisfied with relationships in her life. She was a childless widow who had nursed her husband in his last illness, and since his death she had become very lonely. She wanted companionship and a possible romantic partner, but seemed unable to find one. She soon began to blame her job as the reason for her loneliness and planned to take early retirement as soon as she could.

Within three months, Marilyn retired. Unfortunately, the bliss she sought did not materialize. Instead, she faced her same relationship dilemma, but without even the social outlet that her work had previously provided. She'd been better off at work.

Unfortunately, retirement doesn't fix your life or make everything perfect. Nor does it turn us into new persons. The person I take into retirement is the same me I've been living with all along. We alone decide how happy we will be. Using retirement as an external event to lift us out of ourselves or remove unhappiness is not only misguided but will make us feel even worse.

Once again this points to the conclusion that we need more than financial planning for retirement. Retirement is a spiritual journey rather than a simple transition. It challenges us to listen to the sounds of our souls, to open ourselves more fully to the power of patience, faith, stamina, and steadfastness. (For additional discussion of retirement as a spiritual journey, see chapter 13.)

One of the first challenges in planning for retirement is to replace the nonfinancial rewards of your work. Some of the specific benefits of working life include the following:

- Practicing a skill
- Ability to contribute to society
- Physical work space to call your own
- A schedule that framed your life
- A sense of teamwork
- Some of your best friends
- Lots of acquaintances
- Praise/feedback from superiors
- Sense of recognition
- Socializing outside work
- Goals to strive for
- Respect of your colleagues
- A meaning or purpose that sustains your life

Which of these benefits are still important to you? Which ones will you need to replace? Which benefits will you miss the most after you retire?

Can you, in fact, replace these benefits after you retire? For example, if you will miss "lots of acquaintances" or "some of your best friends," think of ways you might maintain those friendships or develop new ones. You might, for instance, plan dinner parties or host reunions for your old friends and join a social organization to make new contacts.

Use the following space to write about your four top-ranked work benefits and how you will replace or keep them alive after you retire.

1. _____

2. _____

3. _____

4. _____

For many people, the chief enemies of a happy retirement are isolation and its companions, loneliness and boredom. Ironically, the freedom and gift of time that retirement offers us can also work against our opportunities to grow and develop new contacts. Relationships become important, not just to meet your current social needs but also as part of your future. You need to know that retirement will not isolate you from the world.

WARNING SIGNS OF RETIREMENT STRESS

There are a number of warning signs that show how retirement can bring stress into our lives. The first stressor is poor adjustment to retirement and it can be indicated by the very length of your adjustment. As we learned in chapter 3, working through all the stages of retirement usually takes from six to nine months on average. If this process takes longer than a year for you or a loved one, you might want to see a retirement counselor to get back on track.

Another warning sign of stress is a feeling of sadness or loss, an attempt to "fill the time" with trivia that neither enriches your soul nor satisfies you. Since retirement is by its nature unstructured, it will help you to plan at least a loose schedule of day-to-day activities. A structure that is too loose, however, does not allow you to be dependable, whereas a daily plan that is too rigid puts you at risk of losing the benefits of spontaneity and freedom that are so prized in retirement. Balance is the key! Listen to our successful retirees' responses:

"I'm trying to limit structure because even the most enjoyable activities can become onerous if they are too structured or planned."

"Structure is what I am trying to get away from. I don't want each day mapped out with a 'must do' agenda. . . . I don't want to feel guilty if I am not producing something meaningful all the time."

"Every day is a delicious balance between activity and leisure."

A third warning sign of stress is general dissatisfaction with the retirement itself. If you are constantly thinking about work (and how much you hate not working), and fantasizing about your old job and colleagues, then, clearly, you are adjusting poorly or perhaps made an unwise decision to retire.

Another warning sign of stress is increased family tension over your retirement, which may lead to defensiveness on your part and isolation from the rest of your family. Retirement often places a heavy burden on others, including spouses, children, and friends. The change in your lifestyle and schedule may stress your loved ones. They are used to seeing you in one role and with a work identity; the change can be unsettling and even threatening.

The final sign of stress is when health problems begin to occur with increasing frequency, particularly those that are stress-related, such as chronic headaches, backaches, ulcers, and insomnia. As physicians and psychologists often note, the mind sends powerful messages to the body to get our attention.

MORE WARNING SIGNS

Other "red flag" signs that something has gone wrong with your retirement can be predicted by their presence *before* retirement. They include the following negative situations and personality factors:

Uncertain financial status that causes worry and stress

Forced retirement

Retirement earlier than planned that often leads to problems

Resistance to the idea of retirement

Lack of family for support

Marital status (retirees with spouses may have an easier adjustment)

Weak social support network, which may cause isolation

General dissatisfaction with life

Incomplete knowledge about retirement and poor planning

Heavy involvement with work and overidentification with your work

POSITIVE FACTORS

Conversely, a few positive behaviors and personality factors can greatly enhance the retirement process. They include the following:

Positive coping styles: Those who can cope with stress and accept full responsibility for their adjustment do well. They do not blame others for their problems, but seek and use positive strategies to solve problems.

Acceptance of challenge: Those retirees who see retirement as a positive challenge to their resources and planning gain a higher quality of life.

Optimism and anticipation: People who look forward to the next opportunities and stage of life fare better than pessimists. Also, those retirees whose jobs were stressful tend to realize they will have less stress when retired.[2]

These 3 positive factors and the previous 10 negative personality factors offer clues as to whether a retiree can expect a satisfied or troubled retirement. Does the current research suggest any skills that are needed to create a successful retirement? Both the results of psychological and vocational research and my own informal survey suggest seven skills or behaviors that will enhance your own retirement. They are listed (in no particular order) below.

Be proactive. Seek out all the information you can on retirement and plan carefully, not only for your financial future, but also for your emotional future.

Welcome change, stay flexible, and adapt to change. This skill prepares us to seek out and welcome the challenge of the new and to gain a richer life.

Learn to have fun. Make good use of leisure to rejuvenate your body, stimulate your mind, and enrich your soul.

Discover or construct a meaningful purpose for this stage of life.

Live in the NOW rather than the past or future. Experience the fullness of your life as it is now.

Be optimistic. Be hopeful. See the positive in every situation and expect the best from retirement.

Listen to your "still small voice," to your soul.

Each of these behaviors for enhancing retirement will be discussed in detail in other chapters of this book. For now, it is enough to know that we can indeed prepare for our own success in retirement by gauging our happiness now and cultivating the qualities that make for success in retirement.

Points to Remember

- Your general level of life satisfaction (or dissatisfaction) will probably continue in retirement.
- You can, to a large degree, predict and control your happiness in retirement.
- Happiness is an inside job.
- Be aware of—and deal with—the signs of poor adjustment.
- Positive coping styles and flexibility contribute to success and happiness in retirement.

NOTES

1. Coined by Richard P. Johnson in *Creating a Successful Retirement*, 48.
2. Factors discussed by The Everyday Psychologist, in *The Psychology of Retirement*, 22–27.

11

⁂

Flunking Retirement: When Things Don't Work Out

Work does more than get us our living; it gets us our life.
—Henry Ford

People are retiring earlier and earlier. Today, the average person begins retirement around age 58, unheard of only two decades ago. What accounts for this dramatic shift, which is having an enormous impact on our economy and social landscape? A notable trend in large corporations has been the "early out." Retirement windows, early retirement eligibility programs, and attractive buyout packages have the same goal: to dramatically and drastically reduce the workforce. These economy-driven moves have caused both a reduction in the retirement age (sometimes called the first retirement) and an increase in the numbers of retirees who had not planned on retiring so soon. There is also the issue of military retirement. When someone enlists at age 18 or 19, he (or she) can serve 25 years and retire at age 43, with the option of either finding a job or retiring for up to 40 years.

Many of these unwilling retirees are catapulted into a retirement that was not of their own planning, even though it might present a very attractive choice. Life after retirement is thus a rude awakening. These early retirees may not have been psychologically prepared to retire, and they face a huge span of unstructured time. They have too much leisure. Particularly for hard-driving, Type A executives, this can be a harsh adjustment. Do you remember Bob from chapter 1? He admits:

I retired by choice but because my options became unattractive to me

. . . my first year was terrible. I tried to play more sports but I don't like to play golf every day and can't do it anyway with a bad back. Then I volunteered for several things but did not find any of them or the total of them to create a satisfactory life for me.

Since his spouse was still working, he felt doubly bereft. "The worst part of retirement was being alone at home between my sports and volunteer events." He came to the conclusion that retirement was not for him.

But even those who voluntarily choose and plan the timing of their own retirement are not immune to the possibility to flunking retirement. As we noted before, men are particularly prone to finding retirement difficult. One retired wife in my survey, whose husband has also retired, described this situation:

Almost all the men I know have returned to some part-time or pro bono work. One male friend returned to part-time work when he realized that his only accomplishment of the day was to read the newspaper.

A retired woman confessed:

I felt at "loose ends" my first year. I had great difficulty making good use of my time and never felt well organized. This year is better. For one thing, I have relaxed and allowed myself the reward of not being organized every moment and let some flexibility and surprise enter my life.

There are, it seems, several ways to flunk retirement, and sometimes a recent retiree does not even recognize the problem. The seven major areas of failure in retirement are (1) lack of purpose, (2) too much activity, (3) absence of time pressure, (4) identity issues, (5) self-esteem problems, (6) failure to detach from the past, and (7) failure to adjust to sudden dislocation. Let's examine each of these problem areas in some detail.

(1) LACK OF PURPOSE

Sometimes the problem is obvious: there's just not enough to do. We have already noted the importance of purpose and meaning in our lives and how work often gives us apparent meaning and purpose by filling our days with appropriate (and rewarded) activity.

(2) TOO MUCH ACTIVITY

In one sense, even people who do not work in retirement seem to work *at* retirement. As anthropologists have noted, we Americans are known for our earnestness. We work hard even at having fun.[1] As he reflected on retirement role models, one of my retired respondents discussed an acquaintance:

> [He] had sold his business at 50 and seemed to have an active, varied life with tennis, polo, flying, etcetera. Ironically, he has now become a driven computer businessman and lives in front of his screen to the exclusion of all else.

This respondent observed, "If you have to work so hard at it, maybe you should go back to work." His acquaintance did.

Many retirees seem to live out "the default option," which is to spend their days in accordance with a routine instead of a sense of some larger purpose. Many of us know people who have done this. As one of my survey respondents commented, "They have simply built their life around living it." For many of us, however, such a life would not be satisfactory or meaningful. I suspect that we might feel that we had misused the gift that is retirement.

(3) ABSENCE OF TIME PRESSURE

Another way of flunking retirement is not being able to adjust to the absence of a daily schedule. Many retirees miss having time pressure. Everett Thompson, past president of an engineering firm, provides an example of this point. When he retired and sold his interest in the business, he decided that he would try a year without going to work and give full rein to his hobbies, photography and woodworking. This lasted about seven months. As he said:

> I discovered that—unless I had pressure on my time—I didn't get anything done. When I had no structure in my life, I just drifted: got up late, picked up the mail, and so forth. The days went by, but I wasn't happy. Pressure on my time makes everything work for me. When I am busy, my hobbies become more interesting because they are providing a change of pace.[2]

For Thompson, retirement without a schedule was not satisfactory, and he had to take some action. (We'll come back to his story in the next chapter to see how he resolved his dilemma.)

(4) IDENTITY ISSUES AND (5) SELF-ESTEEM PROBLEMS

One of the most common failures in adjusting to retirement is feeling a loss of self-esteem because we have not created a new and fulfilling identity beyond work. As already noted in chapter 5, a sense of identity is important to adults, and work plays a crucial role in creating and maintaining a wholesome sense of identity. Your identity is not lost when you give up full-time work, but it needs to be redefined and re-adjusted to fit your life's new realities. As one retired professional woman who successfully made the adjustment says, "My self-image is certainly tied to what I do. This has not changed very much because I continue to use the same skills in a wider universe."

(6) FAILURE TO DETACH FROM THE PAST

This area of flunking retirement is simply an inability to let go of the workplace or workplace identity. Many of us know or have heard of a former employee who keeps showing up or hanging around the office and who cannot seem to move on—either physically or psychologically. Of course, it's appropriate to keep up our colleagues' friendships, but the main thrust of life in retirement should be on the present, not the past.

(7) FAILURE TO ADJUST TO SUDDEN DISLOCATION

The opposite problem arises when a recent retiree makes a drastic move to a new location without much forethought or planning, suddenly leaving the area where he has spent most or all of a lifetime. As you might expect, such a person will probably experience loneliness, stress, and even a sense of alienation from the mainstream of life.

Moving to a New Home after Retirement

One of the most daunting difficulties encountered during retirement is a sudden move to a new community or even another part of the world. This is not the same as a carefully planned move to a familiar com-munity, perhaps a return to a former hometown or a much-loved summer or winter retreat, but something very different—a sudden, dislocating move to a completely new area with an accompanying loss of familiar friends and community. People often underestimate the importance of the familiar, particularly upon entering a new stage of life. One retiree in my survey was surprised to find:

> We had always fantasized about moving to a new area when we retired, but we had never really done much planning other than researching the cost of living, housing availability, etc. . . . It sounded good to make a new beginning in a new place—and it was. But not at first. The first two years were hard; we missed our extended family and our network of friends. We eventually made new ones, but it was hard to leave the old life behind, harder than I thought.

For many others, a more gradual move makes sense, transitioning to a new area over a period of months, or even years, during which time they nurture contacts and a social network in the new community and decide if it would truly be a good place to live. Because retirement can be a time of emotional fragility, it's good to have familiar elements to help navigate the changes.

The decision to move or not is both a major decision and a very personal one. Your current home may well be psychologically, physically, and financially comfortable, and your surroundings familiar and full of wonderful memories. Nearby friends or family also offer emotional support and are part of a comfortable geographical landscape. If where you now live is comfortable, manageable, and affordable, why move? Certainly not just because you think you ought to move!

Many retirees have legitimate reasons for moving. They may be seeking a better climate, closer proximity to family or friends, new sights, a change of pace, a community geared to an older population, or a smaller and more manageable home. If you are considering a move after you retire, be sure to think carefully and give honest answers to the following questions. (You may find it helpful to write your answers in a journal, as suggested by Rich, Sampson, and Fetherling in *The Healing Journey through Retirement*.)

1. Are you considering moving? Why?
2. Is moving what you want to do, or do you feel you must move?
3. What are the advantages and disadvantages of staying where you are?
4. What would be some of the advantages or disadvantages of moving?

5. What do you want or need in a living community? Consider the following:

- Cost of living
- Arts and culture
- Community
- Entertainment
- Medical facilities
- Family and/or friends nearby
- Opportunity for community involvement
- Recreation and sports
- Restaurants
- Physical environment
- Religious opportunities
- Part-time work opportunities

6. If you are married, are your answers from question 5 compatible with your spouse's? (It would be helpful to ask your spouse to answer question 5 independently.)

7. How well is your current home situation meeting the needs you identified in question 5?

8. If you move, what will you lose or leave behind that you will miss?

9. If you move, what will you gain?

10. Do you have a specific geographical location in mind?[3]

Your answers to these questions will be personal and unique to your situation. The familiar bromides (stay close to family members, remain in familiar surroundings, etc.) are not always helpful and must be strongly resisted. Think about your own emotional and social needs, and try to resist the well-meaning (but perhaps self-serving) pressure and advice from others.

Deciding to Move

Statistically, more than 90 percent of retirees aged 55 to 65 do not sell their homes.[4] They remain exactly where they are. In fact, despite the stereotypes, older adults are less likely to move than any other population group!

There may be many good reasons *not* to move: roots, family stability, familiar faces, and neighborhood resources, including shopping and leisure activities. Why should retirees go through the stress and turmoil of uprooting themselves, just when retirement offers them the time to enjoy the home and neighborhood associations they've nurtured through the years?

On the other hand, there may be other factors at work, and compelling reasons that make the notion of moving attractive. Perhaps the neighborhood has changed and is no longer as vibrant or attractive; or maybe old friends and relatives may have moved away. The large house that once sheltered a family now sits silent and empty, too large for a single person or an empty-nester couple.

Some design factors of the home may make it unsuitable for older retirees. Stairs, narrow doorways, and tight hallways may become a problem in getting around as one ages. Of course, modifications can be made (grab bars, handrails, and wall-to-wall carpeting), but they are often expensive.

Financial considerations may cause one to move as well. Home maintenance costs (particularly on older homes) seem to skyrocket each year. Even if the home mortgage is fully paid up, there still remain property taxes and insurance costs.

If retirees decide to move, there are many options:

- Buying or renting a new home
- A smaller home
- Condominiums and apartments
- Moving in with relatives
- Home sharing
- Retirement resort communities
- University-based retirement communities
- Naturally occurring retirement communities (NORCs)
- Assisted living facilities (ALFs)
- Continuing care retirement communities (CCRCs)

Each of these options has both advantages and disadvantages, and some may be more appropriate at one stage of life in retirement than another. Let's consider each option briefly:

To Rent or to Buy?

The most basic decision involves renting or buying a new home. Owning a home offers freedom, but renting offers its own advantages:

flexibility, the ability to easily move again, no down payment, fixed costs for the renter, and the fact that taxes, insurance, and repairs are the landlord's responsibility.

However, the renter also has to remember the long-term financial and tax advantages of home ownership. Moreover, renters are at the mercy of a landlord's fairness, promptness, and efficiency in taking care of repairs and other problems. Another consideration is that pets may not be allowed in a rental—and that alone may be too great a price to pay.

A Smaller House

If retirees decide to move, a smaller house may be an attractive option for an independent life. The advantages of scaling down to a smaller property are that costs of living—insurance, property taxes, and maintenance—will all be lower and the resulting savings can be invested.

Condominiums and Apartments

An increasingly popular and attractive option for retirees is moving to a condominium. The purchaser pays the price for the unit (a house or apartment in a multiunit development), as well as a monthly fee for maintenance of the grounds, lobby, parking lot, and recreational facilities. Owning a condominium provides the retiree with all the tax advantages of ownership without the worry of upkeep and yardwork.

Moving in with Relatives

Many retirees plan to move in with relatives, often their own adult children. While in theory this sounds like a good solution, it is fraught with peril. The expectations of all parties involved need to be carefully considered before beginning such an arrangement. While each family is unique, this situation generally calls for the utmost in communication skills, tact, diplomacy, and honesty. Some of the questions all parties need to consider include:

Where will the parents live? In a room, a section, a floor, or an apartment?

Is the living area separate or part of the family's living space? Is there a separate entrance?

How much privacy is there in the living area? How much privacy is expected by each party?

Will the owner of the home charge rent to the live-in parents?

Will the parents be expected to perform any chores?

Are the lifestyles of parents and adult children compatible?

Will they all eat together? Do they like to eat the same kinds of food?

How much time together is expected by each party?

What about schedules—do both parties keep similar hours?

Are the parents and adult children sociable to the same degree?

Are there grandchildren in the house? Will there be friction over the way they are raised or the way they interact with the retired grandparents? Do the grandparents get along with the grandchildren? Do they feel they are poorly disciplined?

Honest dialogue among all family members is required to answer these important questions. Such an open discussion and resolution of these issues is the only way to ensure that a merged household arrangement will work.

Community Living: Retirement Resorts

While most retirees opt for familiar conditions, many join the 500,000 each year who choose to move to another state. Popular choices include the Sun Belt, the Pacific Northwest, New England, and the Rocky Mountains. Many of these seniors choose retirement resort communities, which blend housing complexes with a resort atmosphere and amenities. Retirement communities offer a wealth of activities including sports, arts and crafts, and visits to cultural attractions, along with a lively social scene featuring dinners, dances, and parties. Some communities even contain theaters, hotels, banks, grocery stores, and retail establishments.

Those who thrive in retirement communities are relatively young and in good health. They are active, social, and have adequate financial resources. These resort communities, with their summer camp atmosphere, may not suit everyone. Some seniors value privacy and would probably prefer other housing options. But for those who are extroverted and sociable, such an option may be perfect.

Some considerations to ponder about retirement communities include location, climate, security, and housing options. Location is crucial in planning to move to a retirement community. Decide if you want to live close to family and friends; near a big city with its cultural attractions, spectator sports, and shopping; or in proximity to a university. Also, how close do you want to be to an interstate highway?

Climate is also a key factor in moving to a retirement community. Do you prefer warm or cold weather? Will you be happy with a warm climate year-round? How about humidity and thunderstorms? Have you considered climate changes in your relocation decision? Some retirees become seasonal migrants, attempting to find the best of both worlds—for example, by wintering in Arizona or Florida and summering in Michigan or New England.

Security concerns should figure into a choice of location. Some questions to ask yourself before you move include: What is the crime rate in the area I'm considering? What type of crime (violent or property crime) is prevalent? If you are in a gated retirement community, most of these concerns are lessened.

Many retirement communities offer a variety of housing options and the ability to rent as well as own. You might want to assess the future salability of a house or condominium in your prospective retirement community, since most people tend to move on eventually.

University-based Retirement Communities

A recent and exciting phenomenon is the establishment of retirement communities centered around colleges and universities. This new development (discussed more fully in chapter 8) emphasizes the importance of cultural stimulation and lifelong learning to retirees. Residents have access to the university and university activities, often with no fees.

In fact, some college towns are becoming known as retirement communities, including Ann Arbor, Michigan; Birmingham, Alabama; and State College, Pennsylvania. Two continuing care retirement facilities are thriving in Palo Alto, California, near Stanford University. At the Forest community, located at Duke University, North Carolina, residents can participate in courses and programs not only at Duke but also at North Carolina Central University in Durham, the University of North Carolina at Chapel Hill, and North Carolina State University in Raleigh. There are obvious advantages to living in university-based communities: proximity to new ideas and continual learning, valuable interaction in classes between young and old, and shared activities that help to increase mutual understanding and decrease negative stereotypes on both sides.

Naturally Occurring Retirement Communities (NORCs)

This rather odd-sounding term refers to urban apartment complexes where a community of residents has remained stable over time and are growing older together. These communities tend to evolve spontaneously; although the population is hard to quantify, it is estimated that more than one million seniors favor this kind of living. NORCs acquire a reputation for safety and convenience to the amenities of city life. Landlords often favor older tenants, who are perceived as reliable and less likely to cause damage in a building.

Locating an NORC isn't easy, because they are not listed or advertised. Your best bet for locating them is through informal grapevines, real estate agents, and taxi companies.

Assisted Living Facilities (ALFs)

Assisted living facilities are designed to meet the needs of seniors who need help with daily activities, including bathing, dressing, and eating. These facilities consist of rented apartments with kitchens and private or semiprivate rooms. Services may include transportation and recreational and social activities, as well as medical care and assistance.

Continuing Care Retirement Communities (CCRCs)

A continuing care retirement community offers a continuum of care, from independent living through full-time skilled care. The CCRC is summed up in the phrase "aging in place." To ensure that this happens, continuing care communities provide three levels of housing—independent living, assisted living, and skilled care—as well as a wide range of activities.

So you see, a retiree planning to move has many options. The key to making the right move is to know your own needs and assess your options carefully. (Please see the Appendix for additional resources and information.)

For many reasons, one can indeed flunk or even resist retirement, either temporarily or permanently. If this is the case for you, don't despair. It *is* possible to salvage the situation, as we will see in the next chapter.

Points to Remember
- Even if you flunk retirement, it's possible to recover.
- Seven possible problem areas in retirement are lack of purpose, too

much activity, absence of time pressure, identity issues, self-esteem problems, failure to detach from the past, and failure to adjust to sudden dislocation.

- By planning and thinking through moving to a new area, difficulties can be met and solved.

NOTES

1. Joel S. Savishinsky, *Breaking the Watch*, 149.

2. Quoted in Robert O. Redd, *Achievers Never Quit*, 63.

3. Phil Rich, Dorothy Sampson, and Dale Fetherling, *The Healing Journey through Retirement*, 260–61.

4. Steven Shagrin, ed., *Facts about Retiring in the United States*, 4.

12

⎯⎯⎯∞⎯⎯⎯

Retiring from Retirement:
Plan B and Beyond

Work spares us from the three great evils: boredom, vice and need.
—Voltaire

Is it possible to retire from retirement? As we saw in the last chapter, sometimes retirement is not the best path. When this is the case, the solution is to admit it (not always easy to do in our retirement-happy culture) and then do something about it.

There are many reasons to retire from retirement and just as many ways for the creative retiree to do it. Some retirees need to return to work because they need the income that work provides. Others find that they need the "psychic" income—they miss the sense of identity, purpose, and rewards from a job. Still others are not psychologically prepared for retirement; they need to accomplish developmental tasks before they can move into full-time, active retirement. And then there are those who, after retiring, find themselves seeking new ground for personal fulfillment.

For these retirees, a new trend called a "bridge career" is often the answer. A bridge career can be compared to a second or third career. With people living longer, the years formerly thought as the retirement years (roughly from age 55 through age 75) can now be described as a renewal or rebirth stage. For many people, retirement serves as a wake-up call, a catalyst that stimulates them to discover (or perhaps rediscover) parts of themselves that remained undisclosed or underdeveloped during their busy working and childrearing years. Retirement becomes a chance to reimagine a long-deferred dream or even to create a new vision of what they would like to do. Thus, with the freedom of first retirement comes the chance to try out fresh ideas and perhaps make old dreams come true. Many now have the time, the financial means, and the experience to shape their lives in entirely new—and perhaps unforeseen—directions.

Let's look at Bob, the frustrated retiree we first met in chapter 1 and again in chapters 5 and 11. You will recall that he decided to retire from an executive position at a large corporation when his options became unattractive to him. Rejecting the staff role offered to him, he chose retirement and spent his "terrible" first year trying to play enough golf and do volunteer work to fill his time. But he found both courses of action unsatisfying.

He continues his story:

> After about 18 months, I went to law school out of desperation, thinking of it only as a method of intellectual stimulation and not as a step toward a new life. Luckily, I found I loved the law and decided to pursue work in the legal profession.

His bridge career turned out to be the start of a new approach to life and work.

> I work now because I want to and I feel completely free to stop when I don't want to work. For the first time in my life, I have no long-term plan and no ambition to go on to greater heights.

While Bob acknowledges that this bridge career may be only temporary, he remains serenely optimistic about the future and even about a "final" career:

> For now, I am working as an attorney for a public defender and continuing to live a life of routine outside of that. However, I hope to have a long retirement and recognize that this is unlikely to work for the entire period. When the time comes that I will no longer be able to continue or no longer enjoy the current work, I will make another plan. I don't plan to worry about it in the meantime.

This confidence in the future and his ability to handle "another plan" seems to be the result of Bob's ability to face and acknowledge the fact that his first retirement did not work for him. He was able to devise a new plan. Since he did it once, clearly he can do it again, and so the future holds no fear for him.

Moreover, economic conditions are currently causing many older workers to remain in place rather than retire. Labor force participation by workers aged 55 to 64 has jumped by 2 percentage points since 2001, an increase that is unprecedented in postwar economic history.[1] In fact, according to a 2001 study by the American Association of Retired Persons (AARP), 70 percent of workers ages 45 and over plan to work in some capacity in their retirement years.[2] Perhaps unsurprisingly, most of them cite economic need as the reason they stay on the job. A likely factor contributing to this dramatic change is the volatile nature of the stock market. Uncertainty regarding stock portfolios may cause some older workers to postpone retirement and convince some early retirees to rejoin the labor force.

Many retirees return to work because their pension, social security income, and investments cannot support the lifestyle they want. Others need medical benefits, and some work simply because they find they miss having a job. In fact, approximately 15 percent of individuals over the age of 65 are employed, and they are becoming an increasingly important part of the labor force. According to the Boston College Center for Retirement Research, those who opt to return to work are among the most educated, wealthiest, and healthiest senior citizens. They work because they find they miss what work supplied, or they have discovered a new passion.[3]

For example, an article in the *Boston Globe* profiled a typical group of retirees who have opted to return to work. After working 40 years in the computer industry, Robert Carroll of Salisbury, Massachusetts discovered that his true passion is politics. At 63, this former high-tech planning manager serves as a town selectman. Charles DiPerri of Everett, Massachusetts, a 63-year-old retired maitre d', has started his own business right from his living room—a personal waiter service, aptly called "Charles in Charge." And former bank staff manager Bill Budreau is a justice of the peace in Winthrop, Massachusetts, marrying 30 to 40 couples a year.[4]

The question for retirees is no longer, "What shall I do with a few years?" Now it is, "What am I going to do with a few decades?" notes Diane Piktialis, a consultant to employers trying to retain skilled workers.[5] It seems that living a life of total leisure is not particularly attractive to people who are accustomed to being productive.

And according to Clare Hushbeck, a labor economist for the AARP, because the trend toward work in retirement is such a recent phenomenon, the AARP has not yet had the chance to do a comprehensive study.

However, the surveys we did in the late 1990s showed that the baby boom generation does not plan to retire the way their parents did, perhaps because they haven't prepared enough for retirement or because they see the virtue of keeping their minds active.[6]

According to recent studies by the AARP, older workers offer many positive qualities, including commitment, reliability, punctuality, and, of course, experience. Increasingly, as 76 million baby boomers reach retirement age and only 46 million Generation X and Generation Y workers are set to follow behind, there may well be a shortage of workers in the workforce to fill production demands. So retirees will be not only more in demand, but also more able to choose the terms of their own reemployment.

In fact, up to one-third of men and women take up some type of "job" after retiring. So, as sociologists are now advising us, perhaps the time has come to redefine what we mean by retirement, or at least modify our notion of it.[7]

For many retirees, like a man I'll call Fred, the best thing about his retirement was "unretiring." Life without work was not the life he sought, at least not as a full-time commitment. For financial but also psychic reasons, he returned to part-time work. "The thing is to feel useful," he said, "and feel alive, and be a person others can respect and care about, someone they'll listen to." For Fred, being open to and engaged in the world meant being employed in it. For him, as for many, part-time work was the answer. But there are almost as many ways to "retire" from retirement as there are those who feel the need. Let's examine some of your options.

You can go back to work. This is not as difficult as it sounds. "Work" could mean a part-time, shared-time, or full-time position. Although it may have been a while since you were job hunting, the basic five steps to employment have not changed:

1. Analyzing your situation
2. Designing a résumé
3. Networking
4. Interviewing
5. Closing[8]

The first step is really the most significant: it is crucial to clearly analyze your goals and define your reasons for seeking employment. You will need to give honest, realistic answers to the following questions. It also helps to have a supportive friend or counselor to help you determine your answers:

> What proven skills and abilities do I have to offer a prospective employer?
>
> What issue or field am I passionate (or at least eager) to join or rejoin?
>
> What are my established credentials?
>
> How much and how often do I want to work?
>
> Do I need a certain income, or not?
>
> Do I have any limitations: location, travel, time?
>
> What is my preferred work environment? My preferred company management style?

It is always prudent to develop a job-search plan that considers two or three alternatives.

Second, you must use your résumé to communicate with your potential employers. Since your résumé functions as your advertisement for yourself and is the first way you present yourself, it must be *perfect*. Quality of presentation, arrangement, spelling, grammar, and printing should be impeccable. Make sure you include your job objective and the experience and achievements that will make you an attractive applicant. Resumes can be organized to target a specific position or can be designed in either a traditional chronological format or by highlighting job functions. (See the Bibliography for books on preparing a résumé.) Remember that the purpose of a résumé is simply to convince a prospective employer to invite you for an interview. The interview itself determines whether or not you get the job. If you routinely get the interviews you seek, your résumé is doing its job.

Third is the all-important concept of networking. Most people over 50 who find jobs do so by networking. Instead of trying the want ads, therefore, begin by contacting the people you know who respect your abilities, experience, and integrity. Some important guidelines for successful networking include:

> Be respectful of your resource's time.
>
> Be prompt, organized, and specific about what kind of job or contact you are seeking.
>
> Be prepared with referrals for your contacts.
>
> Try to develop other leads from each new contact.
>
> Keep your contacts informed of the results you are having.

Always follow up with a brief but heartfelt thank-you note to each contact person or referrer.

Who is in your network? Literally, it is everyone you know, including family, former colleagues, lawyers, doctors, bankers, CPAs, friends, acquaintances in clubs or at church, fellow hobbyists, anyone else who shares your interests, your professional trade association, and your job-search group.

The next step is the interview, where ideally you will clinch the job offer. Prepare carefully for the interview by doing as much research on the company as you can. Use information gained from library research, newspaper articles, and former or current employees of the company.

Appearance, speech, and body language are important at the interview. Speak confidently and appear alert but relaxed. You are trying to project the image (and the reality) of an eager, vital professional. Remember, the interview is a two-way street. At the same time the company is trying to find out about your abilities, you are trying to discover what the firm has to offer to you.

Finally comes the closing of the interview. Always end with a positive statement and follow up each interview with a letter thanking the interviewer. This letter also gives you the opportunity to summarize your own qualifications and repeat any clinching points you want to make. When the firm calls to offer you a position, make sure you clarify the following points:

- Health coverage
- Salary ranges and review
- Vacations, sick leave, and educational opportunities
- Profit sharing, job sharing, and advancement
- Travel requirements and expenses
- Retirement policy and plans

Do not be shy about asking for the salary and benefits you require. As a seasoned worker, you are a far more attractive candidate than you realize. If you are qualified for an executive position, contact executive search firms, which are listed in the yellow pages. Be aware, however, that some agencies charge a fee even before they find you a job.

A realistic note of caution here. You may not be able to return to a job at the same level as the one you left behind. Sadly, age discrimination still exists and high salary requirements could scare an employer.

Another way to find a bridge career—and one with many advantages—is to use the option of part-time work, which can bridge the gap between full-time work and leisure by letting you earn some money, stay active, and use your time productively. Because part-time work offers a happy medium between working full time and having time for yourself, it can be the best of both worlds, as well as a testing ground for you to decide whether you want to go to work full time or learn a new field or new job skills. It might be advantageous to consider all the part-time work options suggested in chapter 4.

Remember Everett Thompson from chapter 11? Before he retired, he was president of an engineering firm. After his retirement, he discovered that without pressure on his time, he was drifting and accomplishing nothing. So he decided to do something about it.[9] Everett started a consulting service for architectural and engineering firms, specializing in teaching management skills and strategic planning to engineers recently promoted to managers. His goal is to produce 8 to 10 billable days a month, which means that he travels only about 5 days a month. When asked why he works so hard, Everett replied:

Work is a state of mind. For me, consulting is not work. I'm doing it because I'm helping people and I'm learning from them too. I don't think I'll ever retire unless my heart fails.[10]

Consulting is a bridge-career option chosen and prized by many retirees. Ideally, you will be sought after to use the skills and expertise you gained in your previous career, and you will also have some control over your time and work schedule. You can arrange before or after your first retirement to continue as a consultant to your old firm (on either a regular or an as-needed basis) or you can hang out your shingle as an independent consultant and create your own work opportunities.

There are trade-offs to being a freelance consultant. Although you control your work and hours, you must do (or contract for) your own marketing and be prepared for the ebb as well as the flow of business. Your income may fluctuate, so be sure your finances can tolerate uncertainty.

A more dramatic move in retirement is starting an entirely new career, as Bob did by enrolling in law school after retiring from a successful business career. This option gives you a chance for a complete change, plus the use and discovery of new skills. Some of the most excited and revitalized retirees are those who have embraced the opportunity to try something completely new and different. They are surely courageous risk-takers who reap their just rewards. Many times, they trade their former senior status for the steep learning curve of a beginner, but for most of them, the thrill of learning new skills and mastering a new field creates the excitement and adventure they seem to crave. "My new career at this stage of life makes me feel alive and young," one of my survey respondents confessed. "And my kids are amazed and proud."

A final option for retiring from retirement is the popular option of either starting your own business or buying an existing one. The lure of running your own business is especially strong for retirees who have the capital to invest and the strong desire to be their own boss. An example is Todd, who retired early as vice-president of sales for a large manufacturing company and opened his own travel agency. He bought an existing small agency and, by hard work and his superb skills in sales and marketing, has nurtured it into a large and very successful agency specializing in luxury and adventure travel.

For anyone considering this route, the Federal Small Business Administration (SBA) is a helpful resource. The SBA lists nine characteristics of the successful entrepreneur:

1. A positive and pleasant attitude
2. Leadership skills
3. Organizing ability
4. Industry
5. Responsibility
6. Good decision-making capacity
7. Sincerity
8. Perseverance
9. Physical energy

A tenth helpful trait might be luck. If you want to start a new business, you will want to take a close look at your own assets, financial, educational, and psychological. You will obviously need to understand financial statements and cash flow and know how to budget. If you notice areas in which you are weak, you may want to think about seeking a partner.

You should also consider growth areas in the economy, such as health, nutrition, workforce training, and technology. The trick, of course, is to be ahead of the trend, not behind it. If you are fascinated by a certain kind of business, but know little about it, you might want to work for a while with somebody who is already established in the field.

There are pros and cons to starting your own business. But for the motivated retiree, the advantages can outweigh the risks:

You are your own boss.

Your hard work benefits you.

The earnings potential is greater.

The endless challenges and variety make life both scary and exciting.

By far, the most important trait for entrepreneurs is persistence. People succeed if they never quit trying, if they are willing to modify plans, change directions, try new approaches. The true entrepreneur will try nearly anything just to keep going. The patron saint of entrepreneurs (as well as all retirees) might well be Winston Churchill, who, in the shortest speech he ever made (at a commencement ceremony), said: "Never, never, never, never, never give up."

Points to Remember

- You can, indeed, retire from retirement. Your reasons may be both financial and psychic.
- Some solutions include a "bridge" career, which can be part- or full-time work in a new field, consulting, self-employment, or starting your own business.
- Be persistent in searching for a new direction if one is needed.
- It's important to view retirement as a process with many interesting paths of reentry into the labor force.

NOTES

1. According to a September 2002 study by the Center for Retirement Research at Boston College.

2. According to a 2001 study by the American Association of Retired Persons.

3. Steven Haider and David Loughrin, "Elderly Labor Supply: Work or Play?" Working Paper, Center for Retirement Research, Boston College, September 2001.

4. Brenda Buote, "Punching the Clock, Part Two," *Boston Globe*, 1 August 2002, N2–N3.

5. Ibid., N3.

6. AARP Study, 2001.

7. Cited in Joel S. Shavishinsky, *Breaking the Watch*, 235.

8. For a complete discussion of the job search, see my previous books *Now*

That You're All Grown Up, What Do You Want To Be? and *Getting Unstuck: Moving Ahead With Your Career.*

9. Everett Thompson's story is described fully in Robert O. Redd, *Achievers Never Quit,* 63–65.

10. Ibid., 64.

13

—∾∾∾—

Seeking Enlightenment: Retirement as a Spiritual Journey

To live is to change, and to be perfect is to have changed often.
—John Henry Newman

To see retirement as a spiritual journey may be a startling and perhaps unorthodox treatment of the subject. In fact, you may be startled to find this chapter at all in a book about retirement. We are used to seeing retirement as an end to work and perhaps also to productivity. We are not used to thinking of it as a *journey*, much less as a spiritual pilgrimage. And yet, the common experiences of those who have retired emphasize spiritual issues that surface and come to dominate their retirement process. Listen to the voices of some recent retirees as they reflect on the meaning of their own retirement:[1]

"And for me the goal has been one of balance: finding the way to feed my spirit, my intellect, my ties to the people I care about."

"The toughest, or the most perilous thing about retirement, is that you have time to slow down and reflect. If you view your life negatively, that's pretty serious . . . there's an underlying dissatisfaction with what I've done."

"Retirement is like a progressive illness—*and* a spiritual experience. There's a loss of efficacy, but the moral side grows. This is what allows you to give up control over a lot of this stuff. Now I'm making choices on the basis of values, which I didn't do so much in my youth. I have the freedom to decide how to live and what to live for, and I'll sink or swim on the basis of my decisions."

These three comments show that after retirement we sometimes come to a realization of the spiritual nature of retirement ("spiritual" is defined here as that which transcends the physical, pertaining to our "spirit" or soul—what makes us truly human).[2]

Whether we like it or not, a spiritual thread runs through the fabric of retirement. When we have finished with the world of work, we find ourselves pursuing peace and finding purpose in our lives. This quest brings us to some puzzling questions: What exactly is retirement supposed to be? Is it a rest cure? A new career? A playground? A withdrawal from life? A new beginning or a respite? Retirement, it turns out, is an opportunity for growth, a spiritual journey toward our own transformation. It offers the dual prospect of progress or despair and a path filled with challenges. Walking willingly or unwillingly down this path, we are called to become *more*: more interesting, more curious, more personal, more caring, more meaningful in all we do. These challenges are, of course, spiritual ones. In retirement, we are invited to spiritual growth that can transform us at the deepest level.

In retirement, we are called to expand our capacity for living and loving fully. We receive the gift of time, which enables us to summarize and integrate the meaning of our life. Retirement is the period of life when we view the events, hopes, achievements, relationships, and dreams of our life from a new perspective, free from the obsessions of work that might have previously hindered our spiritual growth and development. Retirement can thus be a somewhat painful time, as we change our focus from "doing" to "being." It becomes a time for shedding some of the trappings and distractions of the past so that we can confront our essential personhood. Who are we, anyway?

To answer this question, we have to go deeply inside ourselves and listen to our own spirit or soul. Retirement offers us the opportunity to listen to ourselves and challenges us to pay attention. It is the silence made possible by retirement that both frightens us and invites us to listen to our true selves—perhaps for the first time in a long and busy life. As Mother Teresa said:

We need to find God and He can't be found in noise and restlessness. God is the friend of silence. See how nature—trees, flowers, grass—grows in silence, see the stars, the moon and the sun, how they move in silence. We need silence to be able to touch our souls.

Just as the demands of a career can make us lose touch with family and friends, so can we also lose touch with our own selves. We are not in the habit of listening to ourselves and trying to discern the still, small voice of our own authentic self. This listening and discerning helps us to nurture our inner life.

Of course, there are many ways to nurture our inner lives— quiet nature walks, talking with a good friend, participating in the arts, and meditation or prayer. But however we choose to do it, nurturing and encouraging the inner life is one of the spiritual challenges of retirement.

THE SPIRITUAL CHALLENGES OF RETIREMENT

As the years pass, particularly the years of retirement, the importance of a spiritual life become apparent. Friends die, energy diminishes, and possessions become less important. The understanding of one's own life and even death becomes a matter of intense interest and urgency. We begin to confront anew the central and most profound questions of existence:

Of what value am I?

What does human life mean?

What does my life mean?

How am I supposed to deal with suffering, change, and loss?

Why must I die?

Because the answers to these difficult questions do not emerge at once, finding answers is a process. The answers themselves emerge only as we proceed through the journey of retirement. We see them as signposts on the journey, pointing us on our way to the next milestone, the next question. We seek wholeness in our life. We yearn to somehow overcome the sense of fragmentation that seemed to fill up so much of our life while we were working, raising children, and doing all the things a busy life requires. We long to see a theme, a unity, a purpose in the activities that made up our life. For most people in retirement, the theme they discover is some form of love—love of life, of family, of friends, of fellow man, of society, and of God, the Being that caused our existence.

In retirement, as all through our life, we are called to expand our capacity for living and loving more fully. There is great hope in retirement, hope for new prospects, new purpose, even new life endeavors for as long as life lasts.

The challenge of retirement is thus the same as the challenge of mature age: to confer meaning on life. During retirement, as the possibility of death becomes more real and immediate, we realize that there is not much time left. If our past has seemed fragmented or meaningless, there is not much time left to do something or begin something that will bring meaning to the present or compensate for the earlier lack of meaning. It is time for a total reevaluation.

Like all transitions, the transition of retirement (and the advancing age that accompanies it) necessitates a letting go of certain roles, structures, and certainties before we can reach out to take hold of new ones. We feel a loss of control over our life, and the realization is painful. As one retired physician in my survey noted:

> After 30 years of working, you leave friends, secretaries, and many people whom [you now find out] meant a lot to you and were constant company and stimulation. It can be *lonely* to retire.

Such letting go is central to personal maturity and is at the heart of spirituality as well. The invitation is clear: I must empty myself of the distracting ambitions and false sense of values that are stumbling blocks to spiritual awareness. I must let go of my control of my life as a preparation and prerequisite to beginning the journey toward God.

But from a spiritual or religious perspective, loss and relinquishment is not necessarily negative. Physical, social, and financial loss can be seen as part of the spiritual discipline of emptying, of letting go in preparation for receiving something more fulfilling. For a believer, particularly in the Judeo-Christian tradition, these losses can serve as a reminder of the fragility of human life. Indeed, this insight into human frailty and spiritual transcendence is central to religious traditions of both East and West. The discipline of maturity (as of retirement and old age) is that one must be removed from power and divested of external social roles. One must turn away from the world's claims in order to be united with God.[3]

The movement from Having (things, houses, professions, even family and friends) to simply Being is a familiar and constant theme in the spiritual writings on aging. The Taoist philosopher Chuang Chou says that nonaction (*wu-wei*) provides the key to our being. The *Tao Te Ching* agrees, teaching that, in the end, the "doer will fail" and the "holder will lose."[4] In retirement and, more specifically, in aging, we finally realize that we are not what we have but what we are.

In the Jewish tradition, Rabbi Abraham Joshua Heschel offers a similar insight, noting that only three things are necessary to spirituality as we grow older: God, a soul, and a moment. If we cherish and nurture these things we can attain what he calls "significant being." When we do, we begin to live out the wisdom of the saying, "Just to be is a blessing, just to live is holy."

Of course, "just being" is never easy, just as life itself is never easy. As Maria Harris notes in a stunning metaphor:

> Being is not equivalent to withdrawal from life. Instead, Being concentrates life in a powerful center point, as a magnifying glass concentrates sunlight on paper, igniting the paper into flame. Being is the state of grace entered by the wise old. . . . who have forgone frenzied activity and busyness.[5]

This paring down and concentrating on the essential may not be easy, but its rewards are great. We can begin to develop certain attitudes that are characteristic of the spiritual life, indeed, to a life well lived. These attitudes are:

Reverence and gratitude

Awareness of presence

A capacity for surprise

Generosity and a desire for service

Each of these four attitudes feed into and characterize the life of spiritual growth and development called forth in retirement.

Reverence and gratitude are the responses of the mature soul in being grateful for life itself, for health, friends, and family. It may also mean realizing that you already have much—in fact, you have everything you need. Living with a daily attitude of gratitude and awareness of the mystery of our own existence makes it possible to enjoy and appreciate all that is to come.

Awareness of presence is simply being aware and alert to the life you are living *now*. Too often, we dwell regretfully in the past or fearfully in the future. Retirement gives us the chance to live totally in the present, to fully live each day by focusing attention on the moment and making each day meaningful. It's as if each day truly marks a new beginning for us in retirement.

Life, even life in retirement, is all about new beginnings, and the successful retiree needs to nurture and develop the ability to discover *a capacity for surprise* and new possibilities. As we grow older, we may be tempted to believe that we know pretty much about life, that we've "been there and done that." However, people who are really successful in retirement seem to relish the possibility of newness and surprise and are constantly looking for the possibilities of everyday life. Their attitude is one of openness, alertness, and awareness.

Finally, the attitudes of gratitude, awareness, and openness yield a supreme quality of the spiritual life: *generosity and a desire for service*. If you live in gratitude and awareness of all that you have been given throughout life, the natural response to that is generosity, reaching out to others to share time, talent, and treasure, particularly with those in need. This is, of course, not just about giving money and making charitable contributions; it involves something much harder and more rewarding—giving of yourself, your precious time and energy. And this generosity enables you to serve without expecting gratitude in return.

In a meaningful retirement, the question is not whether we should perform community service, but what the nature of that service should be. Many of us have spent our career lives as volunteers in one or more organizations, but perhaps we saw that service as an adjunct to a successful career or even as a valuable résumé builder. Now, in retirement, you have the chance to bring a different awareness to volunteering: the simple idea of serving others without any thought of what it might do for you.

Gratitude, generosity, and a desire to be of service give you a chance to achieve a life of goodness, of meaning and spiritual growth. These attitudes lead us gracefully through a life in retirement.

In facing and accepting the difficulties of aging, we are led to see things as they really are and begin to establish a new, more realistic basis of self-worth. We are invited to give up all that is superficial, including the illusions and masks of work, in order to find our truest self; we die to the things of the world in order that we might live for the things of God. In doing this, we reach a deeper acceptance of self. Reputation, accomplishment, beauty, influence, affection, wealth—all of these may have been important sources of self-esteem. But in their gradual but inevitable diminishment or loss, we must find other sources from which we can draw our sense of who we are. The realization that "I am *more* than what I do" is a key insight of human maturity. It is also a central belief of most religious tradition.

Christianity, my own tradition, proclaims that the real basis of one's worth lies beyond one's accomplishments, even beyond good works. Ultimately, it is God's love that grounds human dignity and self-worth. God's love is unconditional, both unmerited and unmeritable. It does not *depend* on what I do or who I am. This Christian affirmation of personal worth is relevant, of course, to the young and the working as well as to the aged and the retired, but its power is tested in a special way in retirement.

PSYCHOLOGICAL PERSPECTIVES ON THE JOURNEY

Along with religious writers, psychologists have grappled with the spiritual issues of aging and retirement. The developmental psychologist, Erik Erikson, describes the challenges of maturity in terms that echo the spiritual themes of retirement. Erikson taught that at three critical points over the course of the adult life span, a person moves into a period of special developmental importance, revolving around one specific issue or question. In young adulthood, the question emerges concerning how one is to be close to other people (intimacy vs. isolation). In midlife, the question becomes the scope and direction of one's concern for the world (generativity vs. selfishness). In late adulthood, coinciding for most people with the retirement years, there is a natural turn toward self-assessment that can lead to an acceptance of one's life as meaningful and also a strong natural resistance to the losses of aging and inevitability of death. Here, in late adulthood, the struggle is between integrity and despair.[6]

As Erikson writes, integrity, the full fruit of human development, is the ability of the mature person's to accept one's life cycle, and the people in it, as something of necessity, which had to be and therefore is meaningful.

This sense of inevitability comes only in retrospect and is rooted in acceptance of the goodness of *now*. The expected and unexpected happenings, the "goodness and badness" of my life, are all related to who I am now. Therefore, I can accept them as they were and affirm that it is good that my life has gone as it has. If my life had been different, I would have become someone different. According to some criteria, these differences might have made my life "better." But I would not then be who I am now.

This self-acceptance brings freedom from the despair that can mar the last stages of life. Such a mature acceptance also implies an openness to change. If my response to the challenge of aging is to try to hold onto the past and its roles, I will fight against reality and refuse to accept change, which can lead to stagnation and despair.

Conversely, if I can accept the goodness of now as well as the goodness of my past life and its experiences, I am open to possibilities of change in my future.

Integrity does not, of course, eliminate regret over the limitations of life and the inevitability of death. Mature integrity remains answerable to despair and regret, but it is also able to maintain the tension between believing in the reality of meaning in life versus feelings of despair. The fruit of that mature integrity is wisdom. Wisdom is the ability to view life and its problems in their wholeness, from a mature perspective. And this wisdom can transcend, to some degree, the inevitable diminishment of old age.

The fear of aging and death is very real in our youth-oriented culture. The institutions and images of our society do not always encourage and support our struggle toward personal integrity in retirement. I noted at the beginning of this chapter that the fear of death gives rise to the need for meaning, and Erikson's philosophy confirms this. It also confirms what we have noted earlier (in chapters 4, 7, and 11)—that the need for generativity, that is, a giving back to life, society, and others, is a prominent need in midlife and beyond. This need to share, mentor, and give back to the next generation and our communities is reflected in the comments of my survey respondents, who said that "giving something to others" is one of the highest values of their retirement. One of my survey respondents, for example, described "the urge to give back something, to pass on something of what I've learned, to make the world a little better for my grandchildren" as "the passion" of her retirement life.

And this discovery of passion and purpose leads to the notion of retirement as a spiritual journey. There is indeed a spirituality in retirement, a spirituality defined by seeking a new purpose and a deeper passion. We are given the gift of time to explore the issues and the emerging wisdom of our retirement years. This wisdom balances the demands of internal and external worlds, a balance that sometimes disappears during our working years but can come into full bloom in retirement as it allows us the time, leisure, and perspective to discover the meaning of our lives.

Because retirement is first of all a spiritual transition (even before it is a shift in our psychological, social, and financial realities), it offers us the perfect opportunity for spiritual development. It requires that we change the *self* rather than the outside world. Here indeed is an elegant opportunity for continued growth in retirement: we are nudged by our spirit to seek change first in ourselves and not in the outside world over which we now have less influence. This means giving up the achievement-oriented mentality of our youth and midlife in favor of an inner focus for change. As one of my survey respondents put it, "Be adaptable. Listen to how others are living their lives and be willing to be open-minded for oneself and tolerant of others."

SPIRITUALITY OF LEISURE

Retirement is also a powerful inducement to contemplation, even for those who don't consider themselves very philosophical or "spiritual." We are drawn—almost forced—to reflect on such issues as responsibility, commitment, obligations, altruism, and relationships and also on feelings of anger, depression, fear, worry, hope, enthusiasm, regret, and gratitude.

Retirement begets leisure and a reminder that our sole purpose in life is not to *do* but to *be*. There is a spirituality of leisure that we can embrace in retirement. Leisure helps us look inward and find the child-like qualities of delight, wonder, and awe that we have not always had time to experience. When we experience delight and wonder, we are enjoying the spiritual side of leisure. Leisure helps us to see creation for what it is and to appreciate the wonderful "now." As an anonymous philosopher expressed it, "Celebration of things as they are is the soul of leisure." Leisure is where we can find a deep well of spiritual refreshment.

On a spiritual level, leisure can connect us to our life's purpose and provide us with meaningful opportunities for making important contributions. Leisure can give us the potential to transform lives and the ability to serve others. It is in using leisure well that the retirees in my survey were able to make their own unique contributions to life.

And so we return to the notion that retirement is indeed a journey, and a spiritual one at that. Retirement is a process, a series of discoveries rather than a static event. As such, it is a movement through several stages. All of the issues and the questions of retirement—identity, meaning, loss, fragmentation, generativity, acceptance, and integration—are spiritual issues. The realization of our limited time, the losses of aging, and the need to establish a new basis of self-worth all lead us on a spiritual journey toward a new identity and understanding of our purpose. We discover that in letting go of much that was our former life, we can begin to discover our real life. Do you remember Bob from chapter 12, the retiree who found it difficult, at first, to give up the perks of an executive position? As he remarked,

Moreover, in your working world, you are recognized as an important person. That is entirely lost and I started to see myself as just a useless old man.

However, he continues:

I find the problem completely fixed for me in my current life even though I don't have many of the amenities of my former life (big office, secretary, organization, etc.). All I find I really need is a sense of purpose and a sense of doing something worthwhile.

The changes that retirement brings can either arrest our spiritual and psychological development (as Erikson noted) or move us to new personal discoveries and a reintegration of ourselves. In retirement, we face ourselves without the burdens and distractions of work; if we stay with the journey, and the fear and pain it brings, we can discover a source of positive power, the path of our true purpose, and the real passion of our life.

Points to Remember

- Retirement is a spiritual journey, an opportunity for growth and transformation.
- Retirement challenges you to shed the trappings and roles of the past and confront who you really are.
- In retirement, you face the challenges of loss of things and loss of control. You face aging and death.
- In letting go, you prepare for your own transformation to a deeper purpose.
- Generativity, service, and wise use of leisure lead to opportunities for spiritual growth, purpose, and reintegration of the self.

NOTES

1. Quoted in Joel S. Savishinsky, *Breaking the Watch*, 3.
2. Here I am defining spiritual in a broad sense, as transcending the physical and pertaining to our "spirit," our soul, that which makes us truly human.
3. Discussed fully in Evelyn Eaton Whitehead and James D. Whitehead, *Christian Life Patterns*.
4. Maria Harris, *Jubilee Time*, 197.
5. Ibid.
6. This section is a paraphrase of Erikson's theory in *Identity, Youth and Crisis*, 139.

14

⬚

. . . And They Lived Happily Ever After: The Good News about Retirement

Who saith, "a whole I planned
youth shows but half: trust God:
See all, nor be afraid."

—Robert Browning

It's never too late to be what you might have been.

—George Eliot

Now that we have looked at the various stages and issues of retirement, it seems appropriate to ask the question, What is a "successful" retirement, anyway?

One last time, let's listen to the voices of the retirees in my survey. When I asked, "How will you know if you have been successful in your retirement (by your own definition)?" each one responded in a very personal way. Here are some of their definitions of a successful retirement:

"If I am happy and feel that I am still contributing to the good of society in some way."

"If I feel content and stimulated."

"If I feel pleased—and I do."

"If I'm able to complete goals and projects successfully, have time for leisure activities and family, and maintain financial, physical, and mental health."

"I wake up comfortably and at peace every day."

"I have a list of 25 things I want to do before I die—my measure is did
I do them and am I happy."

"I am content, busy, relaxed. Initially I missed the structure of work, but
not the imposed restriction on life. Now I have structure and no
restrictions."

And on a more practical level, one man observed:

"If I'm still alive and I have some money in the bank. The alternative to
either criterion are not particularly happy thoughts."

However, this same man went on to suggest that it may not be possible
to apply "success" to retirement:

"Unlike a business career, success in retirement is hard to measure, and
I'm not sure we should even try to do so."

Another man saw a more practical side of successful retirement:

"If my wife and I are happy and we don't run out of money until the day
before the last to die dies."

But most cited variations on the same theme:

"I will feel happy, content, and fulfilled that I am doing something for
others as well as for myself."

"I have already been successful for the past six years. I hope to continue
providing well for my wife and extended family and hope to continue
doing so long after I'm gone."

"If I have made a difference somewhere, have enthusiasm for life and love
and have learned new things."

One thoughtful woman offered an observation about her retired friends:

In my view, people retiring need to be flexible and they need to be able
to adapt to change when often what they want least in their lives is
change. They do have a gift of time (if they plan well and are lucky but
they also know that time is growing shorter and their each hour is precious). There is a bittersweet quality that allows one, I think, to luxuriate
in the time but also know that the end is near. The ones who are able
to actualize themselves in retirement are usually those with financial security and good health—both of which are subject to rapid and unan-
nounced change. In a sense, the circumscribed days can create melancholy

and intense joy. But it takes resilience, optimism, good friends and family, and a sense of humor.

We can draw some conclusions about successful retirees from my small, informal survey. There are also interesting conclusions to be found in some large-scale research studies, which profiled retirees who made a quick, positive, three-month adjustment versus those who were less successful. Retirees who had the best adjustment, according to the large studies, had three things in their favor. First, they had well-developed retirement plans. They knew exactly what they wanted to do and were able to carry it out. Second, they were optimistic, challenged, and positive. They looked forward to the future and saw retirement as an opportunity. Third, they had a realistic picture of what retirement would be like, and had been aware of all the issues surrounding retirement ahead of time.[1]

In contrast, "unsuccessful" retirees in the studies also had several factors in common. First, they had a poor retirement plan—or none at all—and since they had no program, they faced a completely unplanned and unstructured future. Second, their attitude toward retirement was negative. These people refused to see it as a time of challenge and possibility, focusing, instead, on all that they had lost. Third, the dissatisfied retirees had an unclear, rather unrealistic view of their own retirement. After one year, fewer than 50 percent of them had made what they termed a "successful" adjustment to retirement.[2]

Interestingly enough, according to a similar survey, the distinguishing factor between happy and unhappy retirees has little to do with how much money they have. Retirees who seem to live the most energized and interesting lives often live on rather modest savings. What they do have in common are the following qualities:

They are engaged in some physical activity.

They try, at some level, to make life better for others. Rather than being self-absorbed, they embrace some personal "cause," which can include the environment, education, health, community development, or the arts.

They experience romantic love with a spouse or partner.

They have strong family lives, but are not consumed by their children. In fact, some of them are so busy with their own lives and activity that they may have to fend off their own children who tend to see them as baby-sitters.

They have maintained close friendships and are constantly making new
ones.

They delight in being an individual with a strong sense of self and independence. They even dare to be eccentric.

Finally, they seem to share a zest for life itself.[3]

You can even say that successful retirees see retirement as a kind of
career in itself, worthy of the care and attention they lavished on their
earlier careers.

Viewing your retirement as a career in itself gives you several psychological advantages. First, you are tempted to view it as a whole, as an
entity unto itself. Taken as a whole, you can see the spacious quality of
time embodied in your retirement. Second, as my survey respondents
found, seeing retirement as a career can give you a renewed sense of
purpose and motivating energy. Finally, looking at your retirement as a
self-chosen career imbues it with a dignity and importance that deserve
care and attention. You may not wish to take this retirement career too
seriously or to overplan it, but viewing retirement from a career perspective can put you on a certain path and rescue you from what previously seemed to be a state of limbo.

The notion of retirement as a career also reintroduces the notion of
planning. Like it or not, most successful retirees have engaged in some
fairly extensive planning, and not only with a financial advisor. One of
my respondents gave good advice indeed when he said, "Plan your finances and your passions in advance." Successful retirees spent a significant amount of time figuring out just what interested them and how
they could include their interests in their design for retirement.

What is most striking is that successful retirees viewed this stage as
the launching pad for a whole new life. Bob, for example, went to law
school and began a rewarding career in public service law.

EXERCISE: SOME RETIREMENT GOALS

Viewing your retirement as a career unto itself and as the beginning
of a new life seems to be an unbeatable prescription for a successful
retirement. One path to success is to devise an action plan for your
retirement. Putting your ideas on paper is the real beginning of the
planning process. It gives your ideas a certain solidity and commitment.

Assign a major life topic to each section of your journal and start
thinking about your specific goals. Some of the major topics you might
want to include in your planning are as follows:

Finances

Health

Travel

Education

Home

Hobbies/vocations

Emotional health

Spirituality

Social life/friendships/relationships

Marriage

As you think about each topic, write your thoughts down under that specific heading. You may want to add a large envelope to each section to keep clippings or articles that will jog your memory or imagination as you plan your retirement. Ask your spouse to join in this exercise (or to keep a separate binder) and set a regular time (perhaps weekly) to consult together on the ideas and information you are discovering.

If the idea of planning the whole rest of your life seems too daunting, break it down into small pieces. Borrow an idea from Bonnie, one of my respondents, and create a list of 25 things you want to do before you die. See if you can include items from each of the headings of your notebook sections. Do you notice a pattern? What does that tell you about yourself? Can you put your goals in some sort of priority list?

Now you have some goals for your retirement. How realistic are they? At this point, *realistic goal setting* becomes crucial. For example, if climbing Mount Everest is your goal, but neither your health nor your finances will allow it, don't lament your bad luck—come up with a Plan B. (There is *always* a Plan B.) Can you take a shorter trip and climb a smaller mountain, one that is closer to home?

Ask yourself what factors limit your goals. What can you do about these factors? If it's money, can you do a better job of budgeting? If it's your health, is there anything you can do to improve that? Ask your doctor what would be a safe substitute goal. In other words, before you discard any dreams, make sure you've checked out all your possible options.

Now you are ready to translate your needs and goals into specific actions and commit yourself to an action plan. Remember: this plan is not cast in stone. You can change it as often as you like and whenever

Table 14.1
Retirement Goals Inventory

HEADING	GOAL	TIME FRAME
I. Health		
II. Financial		
III. Interests/Hobbies		
IV. Work (Volunteer, Community)		
V. Sports/Leisure		
VI. Social		
VII. Spiritual		
VIII. Intellectual		

your circumstances change. Try to remain flexible and include short-term (weekly, monthly, even daily) goals as well as long-range ones.

What goals or plans do you most want to include in your retirement? List them in table 14.1, in the appropriate spaces.
One of my survey respondents described her successful retirement life plan as follows:

> The definition for success is the same for employment and retirement. I gauge success first by making a contribution and secondly through continual self growth.

For people like her, there is an unmistakable joy in retirement, the same joy described by Carl Klaus after his own retirement:

Now, for the first time, I'm beginning to feel as if living well were all that mattered. Not as the means to an end, but as an end in itself. A way of being that I've never really considered before except in connection with the world of art or the acquisition of knowledge—like a Grecian urn or a liberal education. To live in such a way seems such a strange and extraordinary opportunity—so different from the way I've been trained to be—that I can hardly imagine myself doing so. Yet now that I've come to envision such a possibility, I can hardly imagine anything else worth doing in the time that now remains. It's "the last gift of time" as Carolyn Heilbrun puts it in her splendid book about life beyond sixty.[4]

As one of my respondents said, "For some it's a time they can 'follow their bliss.' (I haven't found mine yet but I'm still searching!)"

This seems a good place to summarize the lessons of retirement discovered and passed on in the cumulative wisdom of all the successful (and less successful) retirees we have met.

1. *Know yourself, your personality, your circumstances, and, most important, your values.* Are you spontaneous or a planner? Are you a settler or a traveler? How important are place and possessions to you? The more you know about yourself *before* you retire, your strengths and weaknesses and, above all, what's really important, the better. All the decisions you will make about your retirement depend on this core of self-knowledge. (Review your notes and insights from chapters 4, 5, and 9 to recapture this information for yourself.)

2. *Come to terms with letting go.* This is always easier said than done. How do you accomplish "letting go?" Recall the stages of retirement discussed in chapter 3: preretirement, honeymoon, disenchantment, reorientation, and stability. Remember that the necessary "letting go" of your former job with its title, prestige, associations, and work friendships may be painful. While this letting go and its accompanying pain is *real*, it is also the necessary sign and precursor of a rebirth. In our lives, as in nature, something old has to be cleared away, lost, shed, or "let go" before something new can come to take its place. You have to make room in your life for the next stage by letting go of whatever no longer fits the new structure of your life as you envision it. Can you see an opportunity to take a new path? Are there new interests and new adventures and even new relationships to be discovered? Just as the garden has to be cleared of its winter debris before spring can blossom in it, so do we need to clear away, as gracefully as possible, what is getting in the way of what comes next. The rebirth is always stronger and more lasting if we can honestly face the letting go process of retirement. Try-

ing to cling to the past is counterproductive. We cannot reach out to the new possibilities of life in retirement while holding on to what we had but don't really want (or need) anymore. What is it for you that needs letting go?

And remember: if you let go only of the *externals* of the job situations (the office, desk, materials, and people connected to it) but do not let go of the *internal* associations that cluster around it (the emotional at-tachment to the job, prestige and power, routines and attitudes of your job, your "professional" identity), you have made only a superficial change instead of a real transition to retirement. This process of "disi-dentification," or the loss of and separation from your work identity, is the painful but necessary process that precedes the new phase of your retirement.

At first, this letting go leads to a (temporary) feeling of disorientation, of being bewildered and lost. Be patient. If you are faithful to the process of letting go, you will eventually experience a discovery—the discovery of a new life. The ground has to be cleared so that a new thing can be found or created.

3. *Be sure you are ready. Timing is everything in retirement.* Don't rush into your retirement until you've considered carefully all your options. While it is certainly possible to change your mind after retirement (re-member chapter 11 and those who retired from retirement?), it's always good to time your retirement (if you can) when it seems right to you. We all have internal clocks as well as external ones; trust your instincts, your gut feelings as to the right timing of your retirement. Does this seem the right time (internally as well as externally) for you to retire?

4. *Leave on a positive note.* This means making sure that you do not burn any bridges behind you. No matter how unpleasant your previous job or working experience was, try to remain civil and cordial as you prepare to leave. Not only is this the preferred professional attitude, but you never know when or where in the future you may encounter your former boss or work associates or in what ways you may need them as references or resources. For your own well-being and peace of mind, keep those fences mended as you walk out the door. Be sure to acknowledge and thank your employer for all that you honestly value about your work experience, and then keep a tactful silence.

5. *Find your passion—whatever it is—and invest in it.* This is, of course, one of the most important pieces of advice given by my survey respon-dents. Discovering your passion (gardening, painting, writing, making miniatures, working with computers, or helping in clinics or soup kitch-ens) is the surest shortcut to happiness in retirement. Moreover, in order

to take your passion seriously and have it provide a satisfying and re-warding retirement life, you need to invest in it. Investing time, energy, training, and perhaps even money in your passion is a real and concrete way to demonstrate that you are committed to it and to yourself. In-vestment shows that you take it and yourself seriously.

6. *Figure out what "the gift of time" means to you. How would you like to use it?* Time for the retiree, as we have discovered, is a two-edged sword. It can stretch ahead ominously and empty, or you can feel as if you never have enough time to do what you really want to do. Which will it be for you? Become thoughtful and proactive with your own gift of time.

7. *Try to discover (or better yet) to be a positive role model.* We all know how contagious attitude can be. Attitude can make the difference be-tween a positive, energized retirement and a dispirited decline into old age. As you prepare for retirement, seek out and try to emulate individ-uals whose retirements you admire. What kinds of attitudes do they demonstrate? How involved are they? How do they use their leisure time? What kinds of relationships do they cultivate? You do not, of course, have to imitate everything about your role model; focus on the qualities you most admire and want to actualize in your own life. De-veloping a positive attitude can be a lengthy procedure, but you will know you have succeeded when you come to realize you have yourself become a role model for aspiring retirees.

8. *Expect the unexpected. Illness, setbacks, and crises disrupt plans and shatter illusions of control.* The unexpected can, of course, turn all our happy plans for retirement on their heads. Disruptions must be faced realistically. While it is important to plan optimistically for a perfect retirement, we know that life is what happens when we are busy making those plans. Financial setbacks, family crises, illness, and death are very real possibilities that can bring us to our knees. Still, resilience and a positive attitude can help us cope with the difficult challenges we may face. While we acknowledge that we are not in control of our lives and our circumstances, we still need to see the value of strategizing and trying to develop a new plan. Limited and modified dreams are better than disillusion and despair, and even limited dreams are better than no dreams at all.

9. *Relationships matter. Nurture and keep them.* If we did not take time during our busy careers to nurture and invest in relationships, cultivating friends and family can be hard to do after we retire. Remember Marilyn from chapter 10, who retired in order to "fix" her lonely life, only to discover that work had in fact provided her with her only real social

outlet? Marilyn had to make careful and deliberate choices to create and nourish relationships in retirement. In order to meet people who shared her interests, she joined a health club and an auxiliary association of volunteers for the local art museum.

Because she was naturally shy, she had to make a special effort to initiate and follow up on her new contacts, but gradually her contacts turned into friends. At the same time, as a single woman with no children of her own, she began reaching out to the nephews and nieces of her extended family and reestablished ties with them. With more contacts in her expanding social and family circle, Marilyn began to feel less lonely and more positive about her retirement and her life itself. I am happy to report that she is now busier and happier today than the day she retired. (You may want to review the steps for nurturing relationships in chapter 8 if this is an issue for you.)

10. *Use freedom responsibly.* Peace of mind comes by pursuing something important to you. Retirees who are the most satisfied with their lives are those who have deliberately involved themselves in activities and causes that give meaning and purpose to their increased free time. By now, if you have been doing the exercises suggested in earlier chapters, you should have a very good idea of what would be meaningful for you. You do not have to pursue a serious "cause," but it should be something that gives you genuine joy.

11. *Be realistic. Do not set yourself up for failure.* Take your retirement in small stages. Don't try to plan your entire life all at once. And don't be afraid to acknowledge mistakes and change your plans as necessary. A good retirement is a work in progress—constantly evolving and changing to meet your needs.

As one of my friends observed, no matter how much planning and good intentions are present, sometimes the perfect retirement eludes us. She suggested that I include some ideas to help retirees who may have difficulty feeling all right about themselves:

> To let them know that if they have trouble finding a part-time job, if being with their wife/husband more often is not satisfying, if they were forced to retire and feel despondent—they still have value and they can give and receive joy without sitting on the mountaintop.

I can only agree with her thoughtful comment and suggest that retirement does not have to be ideal to be satisfactory, that living with limitations and challenges can bring its own season of growth and even joy. Focusing on what we have instead of what is lost can be a start, as can looking around us, in whatever circumstances, to see what we can do to help ourselves and others.

There is a wonderful old Chinese proverb that seems appropriate here, since it seems to describe many of the facets of retirement:

> If you want to be happy for an hour, take a nap.
> If you want to be happy for a day, go fishing.
> If you want to be happy for a week, take a trip.
> If you want to be happy for a month, get married.
> If you want to be happy for a year, inherit money.
> If you want to be happy for a lifetime, serve others.

Our retirees' advice and, more important, their examples show the kind of novelty, passion, and purpose that are possible in retirement. Life spans have grown more in the last century than in the previous 5,000 years. Today's retirees can expect to live longer and better lives. Henry Ward Beecher wrote:

> Every tomorrow has two handles. We can take hold of it with the handle of anxiety or the handle of faith. We should live for the future, yet should find our life in the . . . present.[5]

You can shape your future, for retirement is a passage from a life of works and productivity to a life of personal accomplishment, leisure, and choice. Retirement, for those who plan and nurture it as carefully as they did their career, is not so much a final reward as an open-ended opportunity. As one of my survey respondents put it:

> I think of retirement as a welcomed opportunity to define the last chapter of my life.

Points to Remember

- Retirees who adjust best have well-developed retirement plans. They are optimistic, challenged, positive, and realistic.
- Viewing retirement as a career can give you energy and purpose. It encourages you to nurture your new retirement career with care.
- An action plan for your retirement is a useful tool.
- Passion and purpose can lead to a second beginning in retirement.

NOTES

1. Cited in The Everyday Psychologist *The Psychology of Retirement*, 27.
2. Ibid., 28.
3. Ralph Warner, *Get A Life*, 136.
4. Carl H. Klaus, *Taking Retirement*, 162.
5. Quoted in Phil Rich, Dorothy Sampson, and Dale Fetherling. *The Healing Journey Through Retirement*, 277.

Appendix: Additional Resources for Further Information

Source: *Facts about Retiring in the United States*, edited by Steven S. Shagrin (H.W. Wilson, 2001)

ADVOCACY GROUPS

AARP (American Association for Retired Persons)
Phone: (202) 434-2277
Toll-free: (800) 424-3410
   An educational and lobbying organization with local chapters; a good source for printed materials.

Administration on Aging
Phone: (202) 619-0704
http://www.aoa.gov

Aging with Dignity
Phone: (850) 681-2010

Alliance for Aging Research
Phone (202) 293-2856

American Society on Aging
http://www.asaging.org

ELDERCARE Locator
Toll-free: (800) 677-1116
   National Association of Area Agencies on Aging.

Gray Panthers
Phone: (202) 737-6637
Toll-free: (800) 280-5362

Medicare Hotline
Toll-free: (800) 633-4227
http://www.medicare.gov or http://www.hcfa.gov
  Health Care Financing Administration.

National Alliance of Senior Citizens
2525 Wilson Blvd.
Arlington, VA 22201

National Committee to Preserve Social Security and Medicare
Phone: (202) 216-0420
Hotline: (800) 966-1935
http://ncpssm.org

National Council on Aging
Phone: (202) 479-1200
http://www.ncoa.org
  Information and local referral to services.

National Insurance Consumer Helpline
Toll-free: (800) 942-4242

National Library of Medicine at the National Institute of Health
Toll-free: (888) 346-3656
http://www.nlm.nih.gov

People's Medical Society
Phone: (610) 770-1670
http://www.peoplesmed.org

EMPLOYMENT AND TRAINING

Green Thumb, Inc.
Phone: (703) 522-7272
http://www.greenthumb.org

Maturity Works
http://www.maturityworks.org
  National program that matches mature workers to jobs with participating
organizations.

GENERAL RESOURCES

Consumer Information Center
Phone: (202) 501-1794
http://www.pueblo.gsa.gov

Enrichments for Better Living Catalog
Phone: (808) 323-5547

National Association of Area Agencies on Aging
Phone: (202) 296-8130

National Consumers League
Phone: (202) 835-3323
Toll-free: (800) 876-7060

Yes I Can, Inc.
Toll-free: (800) 366-4226
  Provides products to make life easier for seniors.

Internet Resources

Access America for Seniors
http://www.seniors.gov

AOA Elder Page: Information for Older Persons and Families
http://www.aoa.dhhs.gov/elderpage.html

AOA The Resource Directory
http://www.aoa.gov/aoa/resource.html

AOA's National Aging Information Center (NAIC)
http://www.aoa.gov/naic

Eldernet
http://www.eldernet.com

National Network for Family Resiliency
http://www.nnfr.org/igen
  Information on intergenerational and grandparenting issues.

SeniorCom
http://www.senior.com
  General information on travel, entertainment, money matters, health, employment, housing.

Sixty-Five Plus in the United States
http://www.census.gov/ftp/pub/socdemo/www/agebtief.html

The Spry Foundation
http://www.spry.org

Third Age
http://www.thirdage.com

HEALTH

International Longevity Center-USA
60 E. 86th St.
New York, NY 10028
Phone: (212) 288-1468
Fax: (212) 288-3132
http://www.ilcusa.org

Alzheimer's Disease

Alzheimer's Association
919 N. Michigan Ave.
Chicago, IL 60611
Phone: (312) 335-8700
Toll-free: (800) 272-3900
Fax: (312) 335-1110
http://www.alz.org
    A 24-hour toll-free hotline provides information about Alzheimer's disease and links families with local chapters.

Alzheimer's Disease Education & Referral Center
PO Box 8250
Silver Spring, MD 20907-8250
Phone: (301) 495-3311
Toll-free: (800) 438-4380
Fax: (301) 495-3334
http://www.alzheimers.org
    Responds to inquiries from the public and provides information about diagnosis, treatment, research, and services available for Alzheimer's disease.

American Health Assistance Foundation
15825 Shady Grove Rd., Suite 140
Rockville, MD 20850
Phone: (301) 948-3244
Toll-free: (800) 437-2423
Fax: (301) 258-9454
http://www.ahaf.org
    The Alzheimer's Family Relief Program offers emergency grants of up to $500 to Alzheimer's patients and their caregivers in need. Free publications available on Alzheimer's disease, glaucoma, heart disease, and stroke.

Heart, Lung, and Blood

American Heart Association
7272 Greenville Ave.

Dallas, TX 75231
Phone: (214) 373-6300
Affiliate office: (800) 242-8721
Toll-free Stroke Connection
(800) 553-6321
http://www.amhrt.org

The Stroke Connection maintains a listing of nationwide groups for referral to stroke survivors and their families. It also publishes *Stroke Connection*, a forum for sharing information about coping with stroke.

National Heart, Lung, and Blood Institute (NHLBI)
Education Programs Information Center
31 Center Dr., MSC 2480
Rm. 4A21
Bethesda, MD 20892-2480
Phone: (301) 592-8573
http://www.nhlbi.nih.gov/idex.htm

Provides consumer materials on cholesterol, smoking, high blood pressure, asthma, chronic cough, heart disease, exercise, stroke, and blood resources.

National Stroke Association
9707 E. Easter Lane
Englewood, CO 80112
Phone: (303) 649-9299
Fax: (303) 649-1328
http://www.stroke.org

Provides information about stroke to the general public and offers supportive services to stroke survivors and their families. Brochures available.

Mental Heath

National Institute of Mental Health
Information Resources and Inquiries Branch
6001 Executive Blvd., Room 8184
MSC9663
Bethesda, MD 20892-9663
Phone: (301) 443-4513
Fax: (301) 443-4279
http://www.nimh.nih.gov

Free publications include *Alzheimer's Disease*; *Plain Talk About Aging*; *Plain Talk About Handling Stress*; and *If You're Over 65 and Feeling Depressed: Treatment Brings New Hope*.

National Mental Health Association
1021 Prince St.
Alexandria, VA 22314-2971

Phone: (703) 684-7722
Information Center: (800) 969-6642
Fax: (703) 684-5968
http://www.nmha.org/idex.cfm

The Information Center provides written materials on mental health topics and referrals to callers requesting information on mental health service organizations. Publications include two quarterly newsletters, NMHA *Prevention Update* and *The BELL*.

Orthopedics

American Academy of Orthopedic Surgeons
6300 N. River Rd.
Rosemont, IL 60018-4262
Phone: (847) 823-7186
Toll-free: (800) 346-2267
http://www.aaos.org

Information available about arthritis, osteoporosis, artificial joints, and prevention of hip fractures.

Arthritis Foundation
1330 W. Peachtree St.
Atlanta, GA 30309
Phone: (404) 872-7100
Toll-free: (800) 283-7800
http://www.arthritis.org

Offers nationwide health education programs in local communities, including arthritis self-help courses, aquatic and exercise programs, support groups, and public forums.

National Institute of Arthritis and Musculoskeletal and Skin Diseases
Information Office
1 Ams Circle
Bethesda, MD 20892-3676
Phone: (301) 496-8188
http://www.nih.gov/niams

Offers brochures and information on arthritis, rheumatic diseases, and osteoporosis.

National Osteoporosis Foundation
1232 22nd St. NW
Washington, DC 20037-1292
Phone: (202) 223-2226
Fax: (202) 223-2237
http://www.nof.org

Publishes *Osteoporosis: A Woman's Guide* and *An Older Person's Guide to Osteoporosis*. Web site has information on prevention and available medications.

Sight and Hearing

American Academy of Ophthalmology
PO Box 7424
San Francisco, CA 94142-7424
Phone: (415) 561-8500
http://www.eyenet.org
National Eye Care Project Helpline for people age 65 or older to put them in touch with local ophthalmologists who volunteer to provide medical eye care at no out-of-pocket expense.

Better Hearing Institute
PO Box 1840
Washington, DC 20013
Phone: (703) 642-0580
Toll-free Hearing Helpline: (800) 327-9355
http://www.advancedhearing.com/bhi.htm
Hearing Helpline provides information on hearing loss.

Better Vision Institute
1700 Diagonal Rd., Suite 500
Alexandria, VA 22314
Phone: (703) 548-4650
Toll-free publications service: (877) 642-3253
Fax: (703) 548-4580
http://www.visionsite.org
Provides information about the prevention, detection, and treatment of eye diseases.

The Glaucoma Research Foundation
200 Pine St., Suite 200
San Francisco, CA 94104
Phone: (415) 986-3162
Toll-free Support Network: (800) 826-6693
Fax: (415) 986-3763
http://www.glaucoma.org
National peer support network for glaucoma patients and their families. Free glaucoma patient guide.

International Hearing Society
16880 Middlebelt Rd., Suite #4
Livonia, MI 47154
Phone: (734) 522-7200

Toll-free Hearing Aid Helpline: (800) 521-5247
Fax: (734) 522-0200
http://www.hearingihs.org
Hearing Aid Helpline offers information on hearing loss, hearing aids, and locating a qualified hearing aid specialist, as well as handling consumer complaints about hearing aids.

National Association of the Deaf
814 Thayer Ave., Suite 250
Silver Spring, MD 20910-4500
Phone: (301) 587-1788
Fax: (301) 587-1791
http://www.nad.org
Responds to written and telephone requests from the public for information about hearing.

National Center for Vision and Aging
The Lighthouse, Inc.
111 E. 59th St.
New York, NY 10022
Phone: (212) 821-9200
Information/Resource Service: (800) 829-0500
Fax: (212) 821-9705
http://www.lighthouse.org
Provides information on vision rehabilitation agencies, low-vision centers, support groups, eye conditions, assistive devices, and free literature on eye diseases. Distributes the *Lighthouse Consumer Catalog*, a mail-order catalog of products for persons with impaired vision.

National Eye Institute
Information Office
2020 Vision Place
Bethesda, MD 20892-3655
Phone: (301) 496-5248
Fax: (301) 402-1065
http://www.nei.nih.gov
Free brochures on cataracts, glaucoma, age-related macular degeneration, and diabetic retinopathy.

Prevent Blindness America
500 E. Remington Rd.
Schaumburg, IL 60173
Phone: (847) 843-2020
Information: (800) 331-2020
Fax: (847) 843-8458
http://www.preventblindness.org

Issues pamphlets on eye safety, glaucoma, and eye exams. Local chapters offer community services such as eye exams and self-help groups for people with glaucoma.

Nutrition and Fitness

American Dietetic Association
216 W. Jackson Blvd.
Chicago, IL 60606-6995
Phone: (312) 899-0040
Publications Service: (800) 745-0775
Nutrition Hotline: (800) 366-1655
Fax: (312) 899-1757
http://www.eatright.org
Consumer publications on nutrition and fitness for families, women, and older adults, as well as information on nutrition legislation and a hotline for locating a nearby registered dietician.

International Food Information Council (IFIC)
1100 Connecticut Ave. NW, Suite 430
Washington, DC 20036
http://www.ific.com
Publishes bimonthly issues of *Food Insight*. Web site section on food safety and nutrition information has data on adult nutrition, health, and physical activity, including elderly nutrition.

National Association for Human Development
1424 16th St. NW, Suite 102
Washington, DC 20036
Phone: (202) 328-2191
Toll-free: (800) 424-5153
Published print and audiovisual materials on health and physical fitness for older adults.

President's Council on Physical Fitness and Sports
200 Independence Ave. SW, Suite 738-H
Washington, DC 20201-0004
Phone: (202) 690-9000
Fax: (202) 690-5211
http://www.fitness.gov
Distributes information about health-related benefits of regular exercise. Publications include *Pep Up Your Life,* a fitness book for older people, and *The Nolan Ryan Fitness Guide* for adults 40 and over.

Internet

The American Council on Exercise Fit Facts
http://www.acefitness.org/fitfacts

Fit facts, such as *Exercising with a Health Challenge* and *Exercise and Arthritis*.

Nutrition Navigator
http://www.navigator.tufts.edu
  Tufts University's guide to nutrition Web sites includes focus on senior health and fitness.

Physical Activity and Health for Older Persons
http://www.cdc.gov/nccdphp/sgr/olderad.htm
  Summary of the Surgeon General's Report on line.

A Senior's Guide to Good Nutrition
http://www.vrg.org/nutrition/seniors.htm
  The Vegetarian Resource Group provides this useful Web page, including sample meal plans and recipes.

Hospice and Home Care

Choice in Dying
1035 30th St. NW
Washington, DC 20007
Phone: (202) 338-9790
Counseling Line: (800) 989-9455
Fax: (202) 338-0242
http://www.choices.org
  Invented living wills. Counsels patients and families on making decisions about end-of-life medical care. Offers publications and services, including information about advance directives.

National Association for Home Care
228 7th St. SE
Washington, DC 20003
Phone: (202) 547-7424
Fax: (202) 547-3540
http://www.nahc.org
  Information on how to select a home care agency.

National Hospice Organization
1901 N. Moore St., Suite 901
Arlington, VA 22209
Phone: (703) 243-5900
Hospice Referral Line: (800) 658-8898
http://www.nho.org
  Offers toll-free hospice referral line and publishes the *Guide to the Nation's Hospices* every year.

Other Health Resources

American Diabetes Association
Customer Service
1701 Beauregard St.
Alexandria, VA 22311
Phone: (703) 549-1500
Toll-free: (800) 342-2383
http://www.diabetes.org
Offers general information about diabetes and its management. Web site includes recipes for diabetics, research updates, and a list of recognized providers.

National Association of Community Health Centers
1330 New Hampshire Ave. NW, Suite 122
Washington, DC 20036
Phone: (202) 659-8008
Fax: (202) 659-8519
http://www.nachc.com
Offers *Affordable Healthcare for Seniors—A Guide to Federally Qualified Health Centers*, which contains a directory of state primary care associations.

National Cancer Institute
Office of Cancer Communications
Building 31, Room 10A07
31 Center Drive MSC 2580
Bethesda, MD 20892-2580
Cancer Information Service (CIS): (800) 422-6237
http://www.nci.nih.gov
Information about cancer-related resources and publications on cancer prevention, early detection, diagnosis, treatment, and survivorship.

National Institute on Aging
Public Information Office
Building 331, Room 5C27
31 Center Drive MSC 2292
Bethesda, MD 20892-2292
Phone: (301) 496-1752
Toll-free: (800) 222-2225
Fax: (301) 496-1072
http://www.nih.gov/nia
Offers free brochures and fact sheets on nutrition, medications, safety, exercise, diseases, and health promotion.

National Library of Medicine
8600 Rockville Pike
Bethesda, MD 20894

Phone: (888) FIND-NLM or
(301) 594-5983
http://www.nlm.nih.gov
    Web site provides links to resources that will help research health questions.

Prostate Health Council
The American Foundation for Urologic Disease, Inc.
1128 North Charles St.
Baltimore, MD 21201
    Offers general information about the health of your prostate.

Internet

Diabetes.Com
http://www.diabetes.com
    Health Library provides information that encourages educated self-care.

Health Answers
http://www.healthanswers.com
    General health information. Has a section dedicated to senior health topics.

HealthFinder
http://www.healthfinder.gov
    General information on health topics. Section on seniors has links to primary
government resources on health, Social Security and pensions.

HOUSING

AARP Fulfillment
1909 K St. NW
Washington, DC 20049
Toll-free: (800) 424-3410
    Ask for *Housing Options for Older Americans* (D12063).

American Association of Homes and Services for the Aging (AAHSA)
2519 Connecticut Ave. NW
Washington, DC 20008-1520
Phone: (202) 783-2242
To order publications: (800) 508-9442
Fax: (202) 783-2255
http://www.aahsa.org
    Represents over 5,000 nonprofit organizations that provide health care, hous-
ing, and services to the elderly. Home of the Continuing Care Accreditation
Commission. Web page offers tips on choosing suitable housing and services,
and provides a searchable directory of nursing homes, continuing care retirement communities, assisted living residences, senior housing facilities, and com-

munity service organizations. Also offers links to affiliated state associations and information on understanding Medicare managed care.

American Health Care Association
1201 L St. NW
Washington, DC 20005
Phone: (202) 842-4444
Fax: (202) 842-3860
http://www.ahca.org

Publications on choosing a nursing home or assisted living facility, financing long-term care, understanding advance directives, as well as *A Family Guide: Making the Transition to Nursing Facility Life*.

American Retirement Corporation
111 Westwood Pl., Suite 402
Brentwood, TN 37027
Phone: (615) 221-2250
Fax: (615) 221-2269
http://www.arclp.com

Owns or provides services for 36 residential care, assisted living, and nursing care communities in 15 states. Currently building a number of assisted living facilities that provide memory-impaired services.

ARV Assisted Living
Corporate Office
245 Fischer Ave., D-1
PO Box 5046
Costa Mesa, CA 92626
Phone: (714) 751-7400 or
Toll-free: (800) 624-0236
http://www.arvi.com

Nationwide company with facilities in 14 states. See Web site for listings.

Assisted Living Federation of America (ALFA)
11200 Waples Mill Rd.
Suite 150
Fairfax, VA 22030
Phone: (703) 691-8100
Fax: (703) 691-8106
http://www.alfa.org
E-mail: info@alfa.org

The Assisted Living Federation of America (ALFA) is the only trade association exclusively devoted to the assisted living industry and the population it serves. Members include assisted living providers, as well as a diverse range of industry partners and supportive organizations. This nonprofit organization has been developing state affiliates to work with regulators and legislators on the state level.

Atria, Inc. (formerly Senior Quarters)
501 S. 4th Ave.
Suite 140
Louisville, KY 40202
Phone: (502) 719-1600 or (888) 287-4201
Fax: (502) 719-1699
    Assisted living facilities in 26 states. Web site provides listings.

Del Webb's Sun Cities
The Del Webb Corporation
Corporate Headquarters
6001 N. 24th St.
Phoenix, AZ 85016
Phone: (602) 808-8000
http://www.delwebb.com
    Planned adult communities in Arizona, California, Illinois, Nevada, South Carolina, and Texas. Web site offers information on individual communities.

Sunrise Assisted Living, Inc.
National Office
7902 Westpark Dr.
MacLean, VA 22102
Phone: (703) 273-7500 or
(888) 434-4648
Fax: (703) 744-1601
http://www.sunrise-al.com
    Nationwide company with assisted living facilities, including some Alzheimer's, in 22 states. Web site provides individual listings.

Internet

Assisted Living Info
http://www.assistedlivinginfo.com
    Search by state and map for assisted living facilities. Also offers tips on selecting a facility.

Assisted Living On-Line
http://www.assistedlivingonline.com
    An online directory of assisted living and retirement centers by region and state.

Association of Retirement Resorts International
http://www.RetirementResorts.com
    A listing of senior living resort communities that provide on-site supportive

services, such as assisted living and/or nursing care. Includes 11 states and 2 international sites.

CareGuide.com
http://www.careguide.com

Search by state for elder care, including nursing homes, assisted living, home care, hospice, and care managers. Also a resource center for health care information and a bookstore with publications about elder care and retirement planning.

Continuing Care Accreditation Commission
http://www.ccaconline.org

Provides a list of accredited communities as well as links to possible sources of information on aging and senior services.

Guide to Retirement Living Online
http://www.retirement-living.com

Listing of CCRCs, assisted living and nursing facilities, and independent living communities. Information on home health care, rehabilitation, and re-modeling for the disabled.

NorALFA Online
http://www.noralfa.org

Offers links to retirement facilities in the Northwest.

Private Communities Registry
http://www.registryone.com

Private, gated, or master-planned retirement communities in 11 states. See Web site for listings.

The Retirement Net
http://www.retirenet.com

Search for retirement communities. Includes active living, independent and assisted living, nursing care, and RV/resort.

Senior Alternatives for Living
http://www.springstreet.com/seniors

Search by state for long-term care and senior communities, Alzheimer's care, home health care, hospice care, and adult day care.

Senior Living Online Network
http://www.livon.com

Search for senior housing and services by location and cost. Includes independent and assisted living, nursing care, and life care. Sometimes payment is requested.

Senior Selections: Mature Living Choices
http://www.seniorselections.com

Regional listings of retirement locations. Printed color booklets available through Network Communications, 2305 Newpoint Parkway, Lawrenceville, GA 30043, (770) 962-7220

Senior Sites
http://www.seniorsites.com
Source of nonprofit housing and services for seniors. Over 5,000 communities listed.

Summerville Health Care Group
http://summervillehg.com
Provides a listing of its senior living facilities in eight states, including assisted living and continuing care retirement communities.

LEGAL CONCERNS

General

Hotlines

Arizona Legal Hotline for the Elderly
(800) 231-5441

California Senior Legal Hotline
(800) 222-1753

Florida Hotline for Older Floridians
(800) 252-5997

Maine Legal Services for the Elderly
(800) 750-5353

Michigan Senior Alliance, Inc.
(800) 347-5297

New Mexico Lawyer Referral Services for the Elderly
(800) 876-6657

Ohio Pro Senior, Inc.
(800) 488-6070

Pennsylvania Legal Hotline for Older Americans
(800) 262-5297

Texas Legal Hotline for Older Texans
(800) 622-2520
Free hotlines to help older Americans with legal advice on Social Security and Medicare. Services vary. Some will refer you to lawyers who offer assistance on a sliding fee scale, while some offer help at no charge.

Organizations

Better Business Bureau Wise Giving Alliance
4200 Wilson Blvd., Suite 800
Arlington, VA 22203
Phone: (703) 276-0100
   Provides information about charitable giving and avoiding charitable fraud.

Council of Better Business Bureaus, Inc.
Publications Department
4200 Wilson Blvd., Suite 800
Arlington, VA 22203
   Offers information about protecting yourself while traveling, charitable giving, and avoiding charitable fraud.

Federal Trade Commission
6th & Pennsylvania Ave. NW
Washington, DC 20044
Phone: (202) 326-2222
   Offers a free pamphlet, *Telemarketing Travel Fraud*.

National Academy of Elder Law Attorneys (NAELA)
1604 N. Country Club Rd.
Tucson, AZ 85716
Phone: (520) 881-4005
Fax: (520) 325-7925
http://www.naela.org
   Web site provides an online consumer directory to elder law attorneys. Search by name, location, or experience.

National Consumers League
1701 K St. NW, Suite 1201
Washington, DC 20006
Phone: (202) 835-3323
National Fraud Information Hotline:
(800) 876-7060
Fax: (202) 835-0747
   Provides information on crime prevention.

National Charities Information Bureau
19 Union Square West
New York, NY 10003
Phone: (212) 929-6300
   Offers information about charitable giving and avoiding charitable fraud.

National Crime Prevention Council
1000 Connecticut Ave., 13th floor NW

Washington, DC 20036
Phone: (202) 466-6272
Offers a free crime prevention packet covering home security and assault prevention.

National Legal Support for Elderly People with Mental Disabilities
Bazelon Center for Mental Health Law
1101 15th St. NW, Suite 1212
Washington, DC 20005-5002
Phone: (202) 467-5730
Fax: (202) 223-0409
http://www.bazelon.org
Legal advocacy for the civil rights of older people with mental disabilities. Publications include *Elders Assert Their Rights*, a guide for residents, family members, and advocates to legal rights of elderly people with mental disabilities in nursing homes. Learn about the Older Mental Health Consumer Network, an advocacy group that will allow older mental health consumers a voice in public policy.

National Organization of Social Security Claimants' Representatives
6 Prospect St.
Midland Park, NJ 07432
Referral Service: (800) 431-2804
http://www.nosscr.org
Offers assistance in locating representation for Social Security cases. Web site answers FAQs about Social Security disability benefits.

National Senior Citizens Law Center (NSCLC)
101 14th St. NW, Suite 400
Washington, DC 20005
Phone: (202) 289-6976
Fax: (202) 289-7224
http://www.nsclc.org
Serves Legal Aid Offices and private lawyers who offer legal assistance to low-income people. NSCLC will refer eligible individuals to legal service providers in their area. Those ineligible should refer to the NAELA consumer directory.

Internet

Consumer Law Page
http://www.consumerlawpage.com
Offers articles of interest, free consumer information brochures, and a resource page with links to other useful sites. Published by the Alexander Law Firm.

Senior Alternatives for Living
http://www.springstreet.com/seniors
Listing by state of elder law attorneys. Information on living wills.

SeniorLaw
http://www.seniorlaw.com
Access information about elder law, Medicare, Medicaid, estate planning, trusts, and the rights of the elderly and disabled. National list of elder law attorneys on the Web.

Estate Planning

American Association for Retired Persons
Consumer Affairs Section
Program Coordination & Development Department
601 E St. NW
Washington, DC 20049
Offers the pamphlet *A Consumer's Guide to Probate*.

Legal Counsel for the Elderly
601 E St. NW
Washington, DC 20049
Phone: (202) 434-2120
Provides information about wills and probate.

Nolo Press
950 Parker St.
Berkeley, CA 94710
Phone: (510) 549-1976
Publishes how-to books designed to help people avoid legal fees, including a workbook on preparing a will yourself.

Internet

Crash Course in Wills and Trusts
http://www.mtpalermo.com
Also includes information on powers of attorney, advance medical directives, life insurance, and long-term care insurance.

ICLE Online
http://www.icle.org/practice/probate.htm
The Institute of Continuing Legal Education in Michigan offers numerous Web links for probate and estate planning.

Finance

Internet Sites

http://www.401kforum.com
Provides solutions to 401(k) planning.

http://www.fidelity.com
Assists retirees with portfolio planning from Fidelity Investments.

http://www.financialengines.com
Gives general financial advice to retirees.

http://www.kiplinger.com
Covers financial issues of retirement and offers a newsletter and videotapes.

http://www.quicken.com
Provides general advice on financial planning and tax preparation.

http://www.vanguard.com
The Vanguard Group offers an online financial planning system for retirees.

http://www.retirementoptions.com
Provides information on retirement options and gives you the option to complete your own Retirement Success Profile (RSP).

LEISURE

AARP Travel Services
601 E St. NW
Washington, DC 20049
Phone: (800) 424-3410
Offer approximately 250 tours for members and their families.

American Craft Council
22 W. 55th St.
New York, NY 10019

Elderhostel
11 Avenue de Lafayette
Boston, MA 02110-1746
Phone: (617) 426-7788
Toll-free: (877) 426-8056
http://www.elderhostel.org
Offers programs at educational and cultural institutions around the world to adults age 55 and over. Course areas include intergenerational, crafts, performance arts, and active/outdoor.

Higher Education for Older Adults
AARP Directory
601 E St., NW
Washington, DC 20049
Phone: (800) 424-3410

Interhostel
University of New Hampshire

6 Garrison Ave.
Durham, NH 03824
Phone: (800) 733-9753

Offers an educational and travel adventure with an enhanced awareness of other cultures. Most of its 50 programs are international and last for two weeks. Excursions to historic and cultural sites enhance the classroom experience.

National Senior Golf Association
83 Princeton Ave.
Hopewell, NJ 08525
Phone: (609) 466-0022
Toll-free: (800) 282-6772 or (800) 752-9718
Fax: (609) 466-9366
http://www.amgolftour.com

A membership organization for men and women over 50 who enjoy travel and golf. Holds monthly golf tournaments for amateurs at premier golf resorts. Publishes *Senior Sports News* monthly.

President's Council of Physical Fitness and Sports
200 Independence Ave. SW
Washington, DC 20201-0004
Phone: (202) 690-9000

Produces a pamphlet called *The Fitness Challenge in the Later Years*.

SeniorNet
121 Second St, 7th floor
San Francisco, CA 94105
Phone: (415) 495-4990
Fax: (415) 495-3999
http://www.seniornet.org

Educates seniors (50+) in the use of computers and the Internet at over 140 learning centers nationwide. Web site provides online discussions as well as locations of learning centers.

Senior Partners in Education
Family Literacy Center
Indiana University
Smith Research Center, Suite 140
Bloomington, IN 47408-2698
Phone: (800) 759-4723
Fax: (812) 856-5512
http://www.indiana.edu/~eric_rec/seniors/intro.html

Pen pal program that matches seniors with students from kindergarten through teen years.

Superintendent of Documents
PO Box 371954
Pittsburgh, PA 15250-7954
Phone: (202) 512-1800
    Offers booklets dealing with foreign travel, such as: *Your Trip Abroad: Customs, Shots, Insurance; A Safe Trip Abroad; Travel Tips for Older Americans;* and *Foreign Entry Requirements.*

SERVICES

Aging Network Services
4400 East-West Hwy., Suite 907
Bethesda, MD 20814
Phone: (301) 657-4329
http://www.agingnets.com
    Geriatric social workers who serve as care managers for aging parents.

American Red Cross
430 17th St. NW
Washington, DC 20006
Phone: (202) 737-8300
http://www.redcross.org
    Local chapters offer programs such as retirement planning, crime prevention instruction, safety courses, shopper/chore programs, telephone reassurance, health screening clinics, visitation, and home nursing care instruction.

B'nai B'rith
1640 Rhode Island Ave. NW
Washington, DC 20036
Phone: (202) 857-6600
The CaringNetwork: (800) 222-1188
Travel/Volunteer Programs: (800) 500-6533
Fax: (202) 857-1099
http://bnaibrith.org
    Builds and maintains federally subsidized apartment houses for older adults. Also provides travel and travel/volunteer programs for seniors and their families. The CaringNetwork is a fee-for-service program that offers information, referrals, and advice.

Catholic Charities USA
1731 King St., Suite 200
Alexandria, VA 22314
Phone: (703) 549-1390
Fax: (703) 549-1656
http://www.catholiccharitiesusa.org
    Provides services to older people, including counseling, homemaker services,

foster family programs, group homes and institutional care, public access programs, caregiver services, and emergency assistance and shelter.

Catholic Golden Age
RD #2, Box 161
Olyphant, PA 18447
Toll-free: (800) 836-5699
Fax: (570) 586-7721
Helps older people meet their social, physical, economic, intellectual, and spiritual needs. Offers various group insurance plans, as well as discounts on eyeglasses, prescription drugs, and travel.

Children of Aging Parents
1609 Woodbourne Rd., Suite 302-A
Levittown, PA 19057
Phone: (215) 945-6900
Toll-free Information and Referral: (800) 227-7294
Fax: (215) 945-8720
http://www.caps4caregivers.org
Provides information, local resources, and emotional support to caregivers of older people. Members receive *The Capsule,* a bimonthly newsletter. Web site offers a state-by-state eldercare search.

Family Caregiver Alliance
690 Market St., Suite 600
San Francisco, CA 94104
Phone: (415) 434-3388
Fax: (415) 434-3508
http://www.caregiver.org
Supports and assists caregivers of brain-impaired adults through education, research, services, and advocacy.

U.S. Customs Service
1301 Constitution Ave.
PO Box 7404
Washington, DC 20044
Produces a free booklet, *Know Before You Go,* for foreign travel.

Volunteers of America (VOA)
1660 Duke St.
Alexandria, VA 22314
Phone: (703) 341-5000
Information Service: (800) 899-0089
http://www.voa.org
Provides affordable senior housing, assisted living and nursing facilities; nutrition services and Meals on Wheels; home health care and home repair ser-

vices; senior citizen centers and adult day care; congregate meals; transportation; and senior volunteer programs.

Call local affiliate for a list of services offered.

VOLUNTEERING

Corporation for National and Community Service
1201 New York Ave. NW
Washington, DC 20525
Phone: (202) 606-5000
Toll-free: (800) 424-8867
Fax: (202) 565-2794
http://www.nationalservice.org
or http://www.seniorcorps.org

The National Senior Service Corps (Senior Corps) helps people age 55 and older find service opportunities in their home communities. In the Foster Grandparent Program, older people serve as mentors and tutors to children with special needs. Retired and Senior Volunteers Program (RSVP) participants offer their services to education, service, and other community organizations. Senior Companion Program volunteers provide supportive services to older adults. AmericaCorps VISTA, a program not only for seniors, place volunteers for a full year in disadvantaged communities in order to help local public agencies and non-profit groups address community needs. Web site provides listings of each volunteer program by state.

Elder Craftsmen
610 Lexington Ave.
New York, NY 10022
Phone: (212) 319-8128
Fax: (202) 319-8141
http://www.eldercraftsmen.org

The Elder Crafters Helping Others program enlists former craftsmen to make and contribute items for sick, homeless, or otherwise needy children.

Environmental Alliance for Senior Involvement (EASI)
87330 Old Dumfries Rd.
PO Box 750
Catlett, VA 20119
Phone: (540) 788-3274
Fax: (540) 788-9301
http://www.easi.org

Recruits and trains seniors for environmental projects.

International Executive Service Corps (IESC)
333 Ludlow St.
PO Box 10005

Stamford, CT 06902
Phone: (800) 243-4372 or (203) 967-6000
Fax: (203) 324-2531
http://www.iesc.org
Volunteers provide technical and managerial expertise to developing countries and emerging democracies. Most projects last from one to three months. Web site provides list of volunteer openings in the United States and overseas.

Literacy Volunteers of America
635 James St.
Syracuse, NY 13203-2214
Phone: (315) 472-0001
Fax: (315) 472-0002
http://www.literacyvolunteers.org
National program that trains volunteer tutors to teach basic literacy and English for speakers of other languages. See Web site for a list of local affiliates.

Meals on Wheels Association of America (MOWAA)
1414 Prince St., Suite 302
Alexandria, VA 22314
Phone: (703) 548-5558
Fax: (703) 548-8024
http://www.projectmeal.org
Provides home-delivered meal services to people in need.

National Court Appointed Special Advocate Association (CASA)
100 W. Harrison St.
North Tower, Suite 500
Seattle, WA 98119-4123
Phone: (800) 628-3233
Volunteers support children caught in the foster care system by reviewing case records, interviewing adults involved, and speaking for children at court hearings.

National Executive Service Corps
120 Wall St.
New York, NY 10005
Phone: (212) 269-1234
Advises nonprofit organizations, especially in the areas of health care, social services, education, culture, and religion.

National Health Information Center
PO Box 1133
Washington, DC 20013-1133
Phone: (800) 336-4797

Lists organizations and self-help and support groups for getting involved in helping to care for the sick.

National Park Service
1849 C St. NW
Washington, DC 20240
Phone: (202) 208-6843
http://www.nps.gov/volunteer
Volunteers in Parks (VIP) program. Volunteers may work part-time, seasonally, or full-time in almost every park in the National Park System. Web site provides nationwide list of volunteer opportunities, as well as contact information for regional offices and local parks.

Points of Light Foundation
1400 I St. NW, Suite 800
Washington, DC 20005
Phone: (202) 729-8000
Toll-free: (800) VOLUNTEER
Fax: (202) 729-8100
http://www.pointsoflight.org
Connect America program joins forces with other organizations to encourage volunteers to engage in all kinds of community service in order to help solve serious social problems. Web site offers list of local volunteer centers to contact.

SERVEnet
1101 15th St., Suite 200
Washington, DC 20005
Phone: (202) 296-2992
http://www.servenet.org
Matches volunteers with opportunities.

Service Corps of Retired Executive (SCORE)
409 3rd St. SW, 6th Floor
Washington, DC 20024
Phone: (800) 634-0245
http://www.score.org
Retired executives help train and mentor small-business owners and operators.

Shepherd's Centers of America
One W. Armour Blvd., Suite 201
Kansas City, MO 64111
Phone: (816) 960-2022
Fax: (816) 960-1083
http://www.shepherdcenters.org
Coordinates over 100 centers in 26 states that help older adults through in-

home and community services. Volunteers, who are older adults themselves, deliver meals, repair houses, and give caregivers respite. Web site provides updated list of centers, as well as information on how to start a center.

United Way of America
701 N. Fairfax St.
Alexandria, VA 22314-2045
Phone: (703) 836-7100
Toll-free: (800) 411-8929
Fax: (703) 683-7813
http://www.unitedway.org

A national system of volunteers, contributors, and charities that support local community programs. Locate nearest local United Way in phone book or call toll-free information number. Web site offers links to local United Way Web sites.

USDA Forest Service
201 14th St. SW at Independence Ave.
Washington, DC 20250
http://www.fs.fed.us/people/programs/volunteer

Offers information on three volunteer programs, Volunteers in the National Forests, Council on International Educational Exchange, and Volunteers for Peace. Write or call the nearest Forest Service office for more information. Look in phone book under "U.S. Government" and "Department of Agriculture, Forest Service." Web site also provides a Forest Service directory.

Volunteer Talent Bank
AARP
601 E St. NW
Washington, DC 20049
Phone: (202) 434-3219
Fax: (800) 424-3410, ext. 3219

A referral service that matches the skills and interests of people over 50 with the needs of AARP projects, and with other national organizations such as Special Olympics International, the U.S. Forest Service, Habitat for Humanity, and Big Brothers/Big Sisters of America.

Volunteers for Peace (VFP)
1034 Tiffany Rd.
Belmont, VT 05730-0202
Phone: (802) 259-2759
Fax: (802) 259-2922
http://www.vfp.org

Offers over 1,500 short-term International Workcamps for volunteer service projects. Web site has a workcamp directory updated weekly.

Volunteers of America (VOA)
National Office
1660 Duke St.
Alexandria, VA 22314
Phone: (800) 899-0089 or (703) 341-5000
http://www.voa.org
  Service areas include youth, families, the elderly, the homeless, and corrections. Sponsors Meals on Wheels and RSVP programs for volunteers over 55. Contact nearest affiliate for services offered. Web site provides links to local affiliates.

Resource Guide
Volunteer: The Comprehensive Guide to Volunteering Service in the US and Abroad by Marjorie and Adolf Cohen.
International Press
PO Box 768
Yarmouth, ME 04096

Internet

AARP Tax Aid Program
http://www.aarp.org/taxaid
  Free, volunteer-run tax preparation service for middle and low-income taxpayers, especially for those 60 and older.

Impact Online
http://www.impactonline.org
  Provides *Volunteer Match* an online matching service for volunteers and organizations; Virtual Volunteering, which allows anyone to volunteer services from their home or office; and advice on finding the right volunteer opportunity.

Volunteer Opportunities for Older Americans
http://www.aoa.dhhs.gov/aoa/eldractn/voluntr.html

WOMEN

AARP Women's Initiative
601 E St. NW
Washington, DC 20049
Phone: (202) 434-2400
http://www.aarp.org/programs/women
  Call for information on specific topics. Web site provides an overview of women's issues with a contact list of resources.

National Black Women's Health Project
600 Pennsylvania Ave. SE, Suite 310
Washington, DC 20003

Phone: (202) 543-9311
Fax: (202) 543-9743
http://www.nbwhp.org

Provides wellness education and services, self-help group development, health information, and advocacy to black women. Members receive newsletters and educational data.

National Center on Women and Aging
Heller Graduate School
MS 035
Brandeis University
Waltham, MA 02454-9110
Phone: (781) 736-3866
Information Services: (800) 929-1995
Fax: (781) 736-3865
http://www.brandeis.edu/heller/national/ind.html

Promotes the security, health, and dignity of older women. Publishes *The Women and Aging Letter,* a bimonthly newsletter that provides information on health, pensions, living options, care giving, financial planning, and other topics. Consumer booklets on memory enhancement and estrogen replacement available for a small fee.

National Coalition Against Domestic Violence
PO Box 18749
Denver, CO 80218-0749
Phone: (303) 839-1852
National Domestic Violence Hotline: (800) 799-7233
Fax: (303) 831-9251
http://www.ncadv.org

Call hotline or locate a state coalition office at the Web site to learn about the nearest shelter or support. Web site also offers guidelines for getting help.

National Women's Health Network
514 10th St. NW, Suite 400
Washington, DC 20004
Phone: (202) 347-1140
Fax: (202) 347-1168
http://www.womenshealthnetwork.org

Clearinghouse of information on women's health issues. Publishes bimonthly newsletter about women's health topics, including lobbying efforts of the Network.

National Women's Health Resource Center
120 Albany St., Suite 820
New Brunswick, NJ 08901
Phone: (732) 828-8575

Information: (877) 986-9472
Fax: (732) 249-4671
http://www.healthywomen.org

A national clearinghouse for women's health information. Publishes *The National Women's Health Report,* a bimonthly newsletter with information about preventive care. NSHRC staff will perform topic-specific research on personal health concerns, free of charge for members. Maintains a database of health resources. Web site offers links to health resources for women.

Older Women's League (OWL)

666 11th St. NW, Suite 700
Washington, DC 20001
Phone: (202) 783-6686
OWL Powerline: (202) 783-6689
Toll-free: (800) 825-3695

Advocacy group that addresses the concerns of midlife and older women. Publishes *OWL Observer* and *The Field Advocate,* which informs members of public policy issues.

Women Work!

National Network for Women's Employment
1625 K St. NW, Suite 300
Washington, DC 20006
Phone: (202) 467-6346
Information and Referral: (800) 235-2732
http://www.womenwork.org

Provides education, training, and employment programs for women. Web site has contact list of state affiliates.

Women's Bureau Clearinghouse

U.S. Department of Labor
200 Constitution Ave. NW, Rm. S-3002
Washington, DC 20210-0002
Phone: (202) 693-6710
Toll-free: (800) 827-5335
Fax: (202) 693-6725
http://www.dol.gov/dol/wb

Focuses on rights of women in the workplace. Offers free *Resource Kit* of information on work and family; *Don't Work in the Dark: Know-Your-Rights,* information about women's rights in the workplace, as well as other brochures.

The Women's Connection

5030 38 Ave.
Moline, IL 61265
Phone: (309) 762-3940 or (866) 762-3940
Fax: (309) 762-3940

http://www.womensconnectionqc.com

Sponsors events in the Iowa/Illinois area that focus on health or finance issues from a woman's point of view. Web site offers *WomeNews* on similar topics and free online *CyberConnections*.

Women's Institute for a Secure Retirement (WISER)

1201 Pennsylvania Ave. NW, Suite 619

Washington, DC 20004

http://www.wiser.heinz.org

Publishes a quarterly newsletter, *WISERWoman*.

Web site has information on pensions, Social Security, savings and assets, long-term care insurance, divorce, and widowhood.

Internet

MoneyMinded: What Every Woman Needs to Know About Money and Retirement

http://www.moneyminded.com/security/retir/48bklt11.htm

Good Housekeeping booklet. Subjects include IRAs, calculating your nest egg, retirement myths about Social Security and savings, survivors' pension and 401(k) benefits, and protecting retirement after divorce, as well as links to information on insurance and health care, estate planning, and finding a financial planner.

Women and Pensions

http://www.asec.org/wopens.htm

American Savings Education Council Web site provides information and sources about women and retirement.

WomenCONNECT.com

http://www.womenconnect.com/LocLink/MONC/RETIRE

Information for women on retirement planning.

Periodicals

Generations

Quarterly Journal of the Western Gerontological Society

833 Market St. room 516

San Francisco, CA 94104

Gray Panthers News

Membership Department

2025 Pennsylvania Ave. NW

Suite 821

Washington, DC 20077

Harvard Medical School Health Letter

164 Longwood Ave., 4th Floor

Boston, MA 02115

Journal of Gerontology
Gerontological Society
1835 K St. NW, Suite 305
Washington, DC 20006

Modern Maturity
AARP
215 Long Beach Blvd.
Long Beach, CA 90802

National Pension Assistance Project
918 16th St. NW, Suite 704
Washington, DC 20006

New Choices
850 Third Avenue
New York, NY 10022

Older Women's League Newsletter
666 11th St. NW #700
Washington, DC 20001

United Retirement Bulletin
United Business Service
210 Newbury St.
Boston, MA 02116

RESOURCES FOR THE WIDOWED AND THE DIVORCED

http://www.divorcecare.org
 A Web site for a series of support groups and seminars for people coping with divorce. The site also has a search engine for local groups and online resources.

http://www.parentswithoutpartners.org
 A Web site for the international organization that provides resources and ways to find local chapters for single parents of all ages.

http://www.WidowNet.org
 Has resources, message boards, and a state-by-state listing of support groups for widows and widowers.

BOOKS AND PUBLICATIONS

Housing

Dickinson, Peter. *Sunbelt Retirement*. Regnery Gateway, 1992.
Fox, Richard L., ed. *America's Best Places to Retire*. Vacation Publications, 1996.

Gollattscheck, James. *Choose Florida for Retirement*. Globe Pequot Press, 1999.

Greenward, Robert. *50 Fabulous Planned Retirement Communities for Active Adults: A Comprehensive Directory of Outstanding Master-Planned Residential Developments*. Career Press, 1998.

Hayward, J. Keesey. *The ARRI Retirement Resorts Worldbook: Directory of the World's Finest Retirement Communities*. Association of Retirement Resorts International, 1998.

Howells, John. *Choose the South*. Gateway, 1997.

Howells, John. *Choose the Southwest for Retirement: Retirement Discoveries for Every Budget*. 2nd ed. Globe Pequot Press, 1999.

Howells, John. *Where to Retire*. Gateway, 1991.

Howells, John, and Richard Harris. *Choose the Northwest*. Gateway, 1996.

Howells, John, Don Merwin, and Joseph Lubow. *Choose California for Retirement*. Globe Pequot Press, 1998.

Lee, Alice, and Fred Lee. *The 50 Best Retirement Communities in America*. St. Martin's Press, 1994.

Martin, Don, and Betty Martin, ed. *Arizona in Your Future: The Complete Relocation Guide for Job-Seekers, Retirees, and Snowbirds*. Pine Cone Press, 1998.

McGarry, Betty. *Practical Guide to Florida Retirement*. Pineapple Press, 1998.

Morse, Sarah, Donna Quinn Robbins, and Sally Quinn. *Moving Mom and Dad: Why, Where, How and When to Help Your Parents Relocate*. Lanier Publishing International, 1998.

Savageau, David. *Retirement Places Rated*. 5th ed. Frommer, 1999.

Sherwood, Sylvia ed., Hirsch S. Ruchlin, Clarence C. Sherwood, and Shirley A. Morris. *Continuing Care Retirement Communities*. Johns Hopkins University Press, 1997.

Stern, Ken. *50 Fabulous Place to Retire in America*. 2nd ed. Career Press, 1996.

Legal Concerns

Holden, Ronald. *Estate Planning—A Family Affair Workbook*. Family Estate Planning Institute, 1986.

Sabatino, Charles, American Bar Association, and Nancy M. Coleman. *The American Bar Association Legal Guide for Older Americans: The Law Every American over Fifty Needs to Know*. Times Books, 1998.

Personal/Life Planning

Arnold, Suzanne, Jean Brock, and Henry Richards. *Ready or Not; Your Retirement Guide*. Manpower Education Institute, 1997

Ballard, Jack, and Phoebe Ballard. *Beating the Age Game: Redefining Retirement*. MasterMedia, 1993.

Bennett, Robert, and Catherine Bennett. *Retirement Handbook: A Complete Guide to Living Your Dreams*. Melrose Plantation Press, 1998.

Biracree, Tom, and Nancy Biracree. *Over Fifty: Resource Book for the Better Half of Your Life*. HarperCollins, 1991.

Blum, Laurie. *Free Money and Services for Seniors and Their Families*. John Wiley & Sons, 1995.

Brown, Duane. *How to Find Your New Career Upon Retirement*. Vgm Career Horizons, 1994.

Brown, Paul. *From Here to Retirement*. World Books, 1988.

Coleman, Ellen Schneid. *The Lump Sum Advisor*. Prentice Hall, 1999.

Downs, Hugh. *Fifty to Forever*. Thomas Nelson Publishers, 1994.

Downs, Hugh, and Richard Roll. *The Best Years Book*. Delacorte Press, 1981.

Drilling, Vern. *Closing Doors, Opening Worlds: Looking Beyond the Retirement Horizon*. Fairview Press, 1993.

Driskill, J. Lawrence. *Adventures in Senior Living: Learning How to Make Retirement Meaningful and Enjoyable*. Haworth Press, 1997.

Fetridge, Guild. *The Adventure of Retirement: It's About More Than Just Money*. Prometheus Books, 1994.

French, Virginia Robinson, and James C. French. *Avoiding the Retirement Trap*. Acta Publications, 1995.

Fromme, Alan. *Life After Work: Planning It, Living It, Loving It*. Scott, Foresman; AARP Books, 1987.

Goodman, Gloria Bledsoe. *Keys to Living with a Retired Husband*. Barrons, 1991.

Hansen, Leonard. *Life Begins at Fifty: A Handbook for Creative Retirement Planning*. Barrons Education Series, 1989.

Hawley, George. *Dynamic Retirement: A Guidebook for the Golden Years*. Leathers Publications, 1999.

Haynes, Marion. *From Work to Retirement*. Crisp Publications, 1993.

Henderson, Carter. *Funny, I Don't Feel Old!: How to Flourish After 50*. Institute for Contemporary Studies, 1997.

Howells, John. *Retirement on a Shoestring*. Gateway, 1995.

Karpel, Craig. *The Retirement Myth*. HarperCollins, 1995.

Kerschner, Helen K., and John E. Hansan, ed. *365. . . .Retirees' Resource Guide for Productive Lifestyles*. Greenwood Publishing Group, 1996.

Kessler, Regina. *Who Says Retirement Has to Be Boring?* Pharos Books, 1991.

Kimeldorf, Martin. *Serious Play: A Leisure Wellness Guidebook*, 1994.

Lee, Alice, and Fred Lee. *A Field Guide to Retirement: 14 Lifestyle Opportunities and Options for Successful Retirement*. Doubleday, 1991.

Lesko, Matthew, Mary Ann Martello, and Andrew Naprawa, ed. *Free Stuff for Seniors*. InfoUSA, 1995.

Levitin, Nancy. *Retirement Rights: The Benefits of Growing Older*. Avon Books, 1994.

Mesrobian, Armen Z. *Prepare and Enjoy Creative Retirement*. Excel Publishing Services, 1993.

Murphy, John. *The Joy of Old: A Guide to Successful Elderhood*. Goede Press, 1995.

Parmley, Mary T. *New Work Styles for Your Retirement Career*. National Council on Aging, 1997.

Redd, Robert. *Achievers Never Quit*. Thornapple, 1989.

Salend, Elyse, Anna Nolen Rahman, David Harris, Soloman and Marie Bolduc Liston. *A Consumer's Guide to Aging*. Johns Hopkins University Press, 1992.

Schrader, Constance. *1001 Things Everyone over 55 Should Know*. Doubleday, 1999.

Shelton, Phyllis R. *Long Term Care Planning Guide*. Shelton Marketing Services, 1998.

Silverstone, Barbara, and Helen Kandel Hyman. *Growing Older Together: A Couple's Guide to Understanding and Coping with the Challenges of Later Life*. [large print] Thorndike Press, 1998.

A Single Person's Guide to Retirement Planning. AARP, 1995.

Smith, Joseph. *Holidays in Retirement: A Guide to Trips Around Europe*. Foulsham, 1996.

Smith, Mary Helen. *The Retirement Sourcebook*. Roxbury Park, 1999.

Wagner, Tricia, and Barbara Day. *How to Enjoy Your Retirement: Activities from A to Z*. VanderWyke & Burnham, 1998.

Warner, Diane. *How to Have a Great Retirement on a Limited Budget*. Writers Digest Books, 1992.

Wiling, Jules. *The Reality of Retirement*. Morrow. 1989.

Retirement/Financial Planning

AARP. *Planning Your Retirement*. 1995.

AARP. *Think of Your Future*. HarperColllins, 1995.

Allen, Klosowski. *Personal Financial Fitness*. Crisp Publications, 1987.

Bancroft, Daniel. *The Paradox of the Gold Watch—Planning Twenty Years Before Retirement*. Retirement Income Associates, 1988.

Battersby, Mark. *10 Minute Guide to Short-Term Retirement Planning*. Macmillan, 1996.

Baxter, Ralph. *The Arthur Young Preretirement Planning Book*. John Wiley & Sons, 1985.

Beardstown Ladies. *Stitch-in-Time Guide to Growing Your Nest Egg: Step-by-Step Planning for a Comfortable Financial Future*. Hyperion, 1996 (Also available in audiocassette).

Bennett, Jarratt. *Making the Money Last: Financial Clarity for the Surviving Spouse*. Kendall/Hunt, 1995.

Berger, Lisa. *Feathering Your Nest: The Retirement Planner (The IDS Financial Library)*. Workman Publishing Company, 1993.

Bledsoe, John D. *Roth to Riches: The Ordinary to Roth IRA Handbook*. Legacy Press, 1998.

Bogosian, Wayne G., and Dee Lee. *The Complete Idiot's Guide to 401(k) Plans*. Macmillan, 1998.

Boroson, Warren. *Keys to Investing in Your 401(k)*. Barrons, 1994.

Boroson, Warren. *Keys to Retirement Planning*. Barrons, 1995.

Brenner, George. *Plan Smart, Retire Rich: The Book Designed to Help You Reach Your Retirement Dreams*. McGraw-Hill, 1999.

Brown, Carolann. *100 Questions Every Working American Must Ask*. Dearborn Trade, 1995.

Chapman, Elwood, and Marion Haynes. *Comfort Zones: Planning Your Future*. 4th ed. Crisp Publications, 1997.

Cleary, David, and Virginia Cleary. *Retire Smart*. Allworth Press, 1993.

Coyle, Joseph S. *How to Retire Young and Rich*. Warner Books, 1996.

Cunningham, Timothy W., and Clay B. Mansfield. *Pay Yourself First: A Commonsense Guide to Life-Cycle Retirement Investing*. John Wiley & Sons, 1996.

Daryanani, Gobind. *Roth IRA Books: An Investor's Guide*. Digiqual, 1999.

Dickens, Thomas, and D. Larry Crumbley. *Keys to Understanding Social Security Benefits*. Barrons, 1992.

Dickinson, Peter. *The Complete Retirement Planning Book*. E. P. Dutton, 1984.

Dickman, Barry, Trudy Lieberman, and Elias M. Zuckerman. *How to Plan for a Secure Retirement*. Consumer Reports Books, 1998.

Downing, Neil. *Maximize Your IRA*. Dearborn Trade, 1998.

Editors at Beam, and Editors at Morin. *Healthy, Wealthy & Wise*. Jist Works, 1997.

Ferguson, Karen, and Kate Blackwell. *The Pension Book: What You Need to Know to Prepare for Retirement*. Arcade Publishing, 1996.

Gallea, Anthony. *The Lump Sum Handbook: Investment and Tax Strategies for a Secure Retirement*. Prentice Hall Trade, 1993.

Garner, Robert J., ed. *Ernst and Young's Retirement Planning Guide: Take Care of Your Finances Now. . . . And They'll Take Care of You Later*. John Wiley & Sons, 1997.

Godin, Seth. *If You're Clueless About Retirement Planning and Want to Know More*. Dearborn Trade, 1997.

Goldberg, Seymour. *J.K. Lasser's How to Pay Less Tax on Your Retirement Savings*. Macmillan, 1997.

Halman, G. Victor. *Financial Planning for Retirement*. McGraw-Hill, 1992.

Hallman, V., and J. Rosenbloom. *Personal Financial Planning*. McGraw-Hill, 1987.

Hannon, Kerry. *10 Minute Guide to Retirement for Women*. Macmillan, 1996.

Haynes, Marion, ed. *The Best of Retirement Planning*. Crisp Publications, 1997.

Hinrichs, Paul R. *Estate and Retirement Planning: Making Your Money Work Harder*. Now Books, 1996.

Hoffman, Ellen. *Bankroll Your Future: How to Get the Most from Uncle Sam for Your Retirement Years—Social Security, Medicare, and Much More*. Newmarket Press, 1999.

Holzer, Bambi, Elaine Floyd, and Mary Farrell. *Retire Rich: The Baby Boomer's Guide to a Secure Future*. John Wiley & Sons, 1998.

Hutchison, Anna Marie. *IRA Investing Made Easy*. Globe Pequot Press, 1996.

Iwaszko, Knute, and Brian O'Connell. *The 401(k) Millionaire*. Villard Books, 1999.

Johnson, Richard, and Warren Jensen. *The Fifteen Factors of Retirement Success*. Kendall/Hunt, 1989.

Jorgensen, James A. *It's Never Too Late to Get Rich: The Secrets of Building a Nest Egg at Any Age*. Dearborn Financial Publishing, 1994.

Katzeff, Paul. *10 Minute Guide to 401(k) Plans*. Macmillan, 1996.

Kehrer, Daniel. *Kiplinger's 12 Steps to a Worry-Free Retirement*. Kiplinger Books, 1995.

Keithley, M.C. *Retire Early Retire Well: The No Nonsense Guide to Million Dollar Wealth Building Alternatives*. Bookmasters, 1996.

Krane, J. *Can I Afford to Retire?* New Leaf Communication, 1993.

Lee, Barbara. *The Financially Independent Woman: a Step-by-Step Guide to Successful Investing*. Citadel Press, 1998.

Leedy, Jack, and James Wynbrandt. *Executive Retirement Management: A Manager's Guide to Planning and Implementation of a Successful Retirement*. Facts on File, 1988.

Littauer, Stephen L. *Financial Independence the Smart Way: Investing for Growth, Income, and Retirement*. Dearborn Trade, 1999.

Malaspina, Margaret A. *Don't Die Broke: How to Turn Your Retirement Savings into Lasting Income*. Bloomberg Press, 1999.

Martin, Deirdre. *The 21st Century Investor: Investing for Retirement*. Avon Books, 1998.

McAleese, Tama. *Money Power for Retirement*. Chelsea House, 1997.

Merritt Steve. *All about the New IRA: How to Cash in on the New Tax Law Changes*. Halyard Press, 1998.

Merritt, Steve. *How to Build Wealth with Your 401(k): Everything You need to Know to Become More Than a Millionaire over the Course of Your Working Lifetime*. Halyard Press, 1997.

Michaels, Joe. *Prime of Your Life*. Facts on File, 1981.

Morris, Virginia B., Kenneth M. Morris, and Virginia Morris. *Creating Retirement Income*. McGraw-Hill, 1999.

Orman, Suze. *You've Earned It, Don't Loose It: Mistakes You Can't Afford*. Newmarket Press, 1997.

O'Shaughnessy, James. *How to Retire Rich: Time-Tested Strategies to Beat the Market and Retire in Style*. Broadway Books, 1997.

Parrot, William, and John Parrot. *You Can Afford to Retire*. Prentice Hall, 1992.

Petras, Kathryn, and Ross Petras. *The Only Retirement Guide You'll Ever Need*. Poseidon Press, 1991.

Phillips, Lee, and Kristy Phillips. *Protecting Your Financial Future*. Lega-Lees, 1997.

Powers, Jacqueline K., Michael D. Powers, and Stephen Pollan, ed. *How to Start a Retirement Business*. Avon Books, 1996.

Price Waterhouse Retirement Planning Advisor. Pocket Books, 1990.

Price Waterhouse LLP, and Roger Hindman, ed. *Secure Your Future.* Irwin Professional Publishing, 1996.

Quinn, Jane Bryant. *Making the Most of Your Money: Smart Ways to Create Wealth and Plan Your Finances in the 90's.* Simon & Schuster, 1991.

Robinson, Marc. *Managing Your 401(k).* Time-Life 1997.

Rosenberg, Stephen. *Last Minute Retirement Planning.* Career Press, 1998.

Rowland, Mary. *A Commonsense Guide to Your 401(k).* Bloomberg Press, 1997.

Salwen, Judy. *Solo Retirement.* Dodd, Mead & Company, 1983.

Schurenberg, Eric. *401(k): Take Charge of Your Future.* Warner Books, 1996.

Shirley, Kay R., and Anita Sharpe. *The Baby Boomer Financial Wake-Up Call: It's Not Too Late to Be Financially Secure!* Dearborn Trade, 1999.

Silver, Don. *Baby Boomer Retirement: 65 Simple ways to Protect Your Future.* Adams Hall Publications, 1998.

Slesnick, Twila, and John C. Suttle. *IRAs, 401(k)s, and Other Retirement Plans: Taking Your Money Out.* Nolo Press, 1998.

Smith, James. *The Path to a Successful Retirement.* Sligo Publishing, 1995.

Spare, Anthony. *Last Chance Financial Planning Guide: It's Not Too Late to Plan for Your Retirement if You Start Now.* Prima Publishing, 1997.

Staff of Kiplinger's Personal Finance Magazine. *Kiplinger's Retire Worry-Free.* Kiplinger Books, 1998.

Stein, Michael K. *The Prosperous Retirement: Guide to New Reality.* Emstco Press, 1998.

Trock, Gary R. *The Roth IRA Made Simple.* Conquest Publishing, 1998.

Vernon, Steve. *Don't Work Forever! Simple Steps Baby Boomers Must Take to Ever Retire.* John Wiley & Sons, 1994.

Waitley, Denis, and Eudora Seyfer. *How to Be Happily Retired.* Celestial Arts, 1995.

Warner, Ralph E. *Get a Life: You Don't Need a Million to Retire Well.* Nolo Press, 1998.

Wasik, John F. *The Late-Start Investor: The Better-Late-Than-Never Guide to Realizing Your Retirement Income.* Owl Books, 1999.

Weltman, Barbara, and Art Linkletter. *The Complete Idiot's Guide to Making Money After You Retire.* Alpha Books, 1998.

Williamson, Gordon K. *Making the Most of Your 401(k).* Adams Media Corporation, 1997.

Zimmerman, Elaine. *How to Retire with a Million Dollars.* HarperCollins, 1998.

American Association of Retired Persons Publications

AARP Publications
601 E St. NW
Washington, DC 20049
Phone: (202) 434-2277

Toll-free: (800) 424-3410

http://www.aarp.org

To order a free AARP Publications Catalog that lists the organization's most frequently requested printed materials, call (800) 424-3410. Individual documents can be ordered at no charge via the toll-free information line or by mail using the order form included with the catalog. Here's a sampling of what is available through AARP.

Advance Directives

Medical Treatment: Decide in Advance, (D15632)
Planning for Incapacity: A Self-Help Guide, (D14821)
Shape Your Health Care Future with Health Care Advance Directives, (D15803)

Americans with Disabilities Act

Accessibility: It's Yours for the Asking!, (D15520)

Assisted Living Facilities

Assisted Living: Reconceptualizing Regulation to Meet Consumers' Needs & Preferences, (D16261)
A Home Away from Home: A Consumer Guide to Board and Care Homes and Assisted Living Facilities, (D12446)

Consumer Fraud

AARP Connections for Independent Living-Fraud, (D16234)
Senior Consumer Alert—Are Your Donations Hitting Their Target? Charity Scams and Deceptive Fundraising Tactics, (D16616)
Unfair and Deceptive Acts and Practices: Survey of State Laws, (D16027)

Consumer Protection

Consumer Rights, (D15891)
Consumer Rights: Do You Know What Your Consumer Rights Are?, (D15890)
A Guide to Deregulation and Competition in the Electric and Telecommunications Industries, (D13936)
Unfair and Deceptive Acts and Practices: Survey of State Laws, (D16027)

Durable Medical Equipment

Product Report—Electric Scooters, (D15979)
Product Report—Walkers, (D14390)
Product Report—Wheel Chairs, (D14049)
What You Need to Know About Durable Medical Equipment, (D13390)

Early Retirement Incentives

Look Before You Leap: A Guide to Early Retirement Incentive Programs, (D13390)

Employment

The First Step: Getting Started in Starting Your Own Business, (D15084)
Using the Experience of a Lifetime-Update, (D13353)
Working Options, (D12403)

Estate Planning

Life Transitions, (D15870)

Financial Planning

AARP Connections for Independent Living-Financial Security, (D16235)
Facts About Financial Planners, (D14050)

Grandparenting

AARP Grandparent Information Center, (D15212)
AARP Grandparent Information Center (Spanish version), (D16513)
Grandparents Raising Their Grandchildren, (D15272)
Parenting Grandchildren: A Voice for Grandparents, (D15536)
Tips for Grandparents: Raising Healthy Grandchildren, (D15514)
Tips for Grandparents: Starting a Support Group, (D16022)
Tips for Grandparents: Starting a Support Group (Spanish version), (D16725)
Tips for Grandparents: Welfare Reform and Your Family, (D16472)

Health Insurance

Health Care Delivery and Insurance, (D15868)
Reforming the Health Care System: State Profiles, (D16828)

Health Maintenance Organizations

An Assessment of Medicare Beneficiaries' Understanding of the Differences Between the Traditional Medicare Program and HMOs, (D16726)

Hearing Impairment

Resource Guide for Persons Who Are Deaf or Hard of Hearing, (D14925)

Housing Options

Expanding Housing Choices for Older People, (D15819)
Facts About Older Women: Housing and Living Arrangements-Fact Sheet, (D12880)
Housing, (D15561)

Independent Living

How to Help Older Adults in Your Community Live Independently, (D16431)
Information Distribution, (D16429)
Neighbor to Neighbor, (D16430)

Information and Referral Services

Directory of Toll-Free Numbers, (C1172)

Investments

Investor Tips on Understanding Broker Compensation Practices, (D16711)
What Every Investor Needs to Know: How to Prevent and Resolve Problems with
    Investment Professionals, (D15863)

Legal Problems

Legal Q & A, (D15947)

Living Trusts

Product Report-Wills & Living Trusts, (D14535)

Long-Term Care Insurance

Before You Buy: A Guide to Long-Term Care Insurance, (D12893)

Managed Care

AARP Bulletin Special Report on Managed Care, (D16348)
Checkpoints for Managed Care: How to Choose a Health Plan, (D16342)
Consumer Protections in Managed Care, (D16240)
Making Medicare Choices, (D16747)
Managed Care: An AARP Guide for Medicare Beneficiaries, (D15595)
Nine Ways to Get the Most from Your Managed Care Health Care Plan, (D16615)

Medicaid

Do You Need Help Paying Your Health Care Bills?, (D16615)
Medicaid Estate Recovery for Long-Term Care Under OBRA '93, (D16443)

Medicare

Medicare Basics, (D16812)
Medicare Fraud Kit, (D16881)
What You Need to Know About Durable Medical Equipment Fraud, (D16774)
What You Need to Know About Medicare Fraud, (D16773)
Your Three-Step Plan to Fight Medicare Fraud, (D16660)
Your Three-Step Plan to Fight Medicare Fraud (Spanish version), (D16661)

Medigap

Payment Record for Health Insurance Policies, (D13561)
Selecting Medicare Supplemental Insurance, (D16831)

Mental Health

I Wonder Who Else Can Help, (D13832)
I Wonder Who Else Can Help, (Spanish version), (D14946)

If Only I Knew What To Say or Do . . . Ideas for Helping a Friend in Crisis,
(D13830)

Pensions

Fighting Inflation: How Does Your Cola Compare, (D16444)
Woman's Guide to Pension Rights, (D12258)
Your Pension Plan: A Guide to Getting Through the Maze, (D13533)
Your 401(k) Plan: Building Toward Your Retirement Security, (D15975)

Personal Finances

Choosing Mutual Funds, (D16359)
Finance, (D15809)
Living Better on Less, (D14944)
A Primer on Personal Money Management for Midlife and Older Women, (D13183)

Public Assistance

AARP Reach Fact Sheet, (D16682)
Barriers to Getting Public Benefits, (D15738)
Many Older People Can Get Extra Income But Aren't Getting It. Could You be
One?, (D16850)
Public Benefits—Who Gets Them and Who Still Needs Them?, (D15739)

Safety

AARP Connections for Independent Living-Burglary Prevention, (D16233)
Falls and Older People, (D14195)
Fire Safety Checklist for Older Consumers, (D16487)
Home Safe Home: How to Prevent Falls in the Home, (D16598)

Shared Housing

A Consumer's Guide to Homesharing, (D12774)

Social Security

Facts About the Notch: Information from AARP, (D13509)
Social Security and Supplemental Security Income Programs for People with Disabil-
ities: How They Compare-PPI Fact Sheet, (D15433)
Social Security Q & A-Earnings Limit, (D13761)
Social Security Q & A-Earnings Limit, (Spanish version), (D13834)
Social Security Q & A-Public Pension Offset, (D14613)
The Social Security Book: What Every Woman Absolutely Needs to Know,
(D14117)

Supplemental Security Income

Persons Who Are Disabled or Over 65—You May Be Eligible for Additional Cash
Benefits from SSI!, (D14755)
Social Security and Supplemental Security Income, (D15433)

Telemarketing Fraud

AARP Bulletin Special Report on Fighting Phone Fraud, (D16604)
Consumer Fraud: Telemarketing, (D15385)
Consumer Fraud: Telemarketing, (Spanish version), (D16343)
Findings from a Baseline Omnibus Survey on Telemarketing Solicitations, (D16361)
Telemarketing Fraud, (D16540)
Telemarketing Fraud (Spanish version), (D16541)
Telemarketing Fraud Victimization of Older Americans: An AARP Survey, (D16055)

Vision Disorders

Resource Guide for Persons Who Are Blind or Visually Impaired, (D14926)

Volunteer Opportunities

AARP Volunteer Talent Bank-Fact Sheet, (D15049)
Bringing Lifetimes of Experience: A Guide for Involving Older Volunteers, (D15539)
Ever Thought About Volunteering But Didn't Know Where to Begin?, (D12329)
To Serve, Not to Be Served: A Manual of Opportunity and a Challenge, (D12028)
Volunteer Talent Bank Guidelines for Participation, (D12560)

Women's Issues

Women's Issues, (D15889)

Social Security Administration

Office of Public Inquiries
6401 Security Blvd.
Baltimore, MD 21235
Phone: (410) 965-7000
Toll-free: (800) 772-1213
Fax: (410) 965-0695
http://www.ssa.gov

Free Social Security publications are available by calling the toll-free information line or by downloading them from the Social Security Administration Web site. Or, use the SSA's FAX Catalog. Call the toll-free number, (888) 475-7000, from a touch-tone phone and a voice menu will guide you through the steps necessary to receive your documents. You must have the telephone number of the fax machine to which you want the documents sent.

Social Security Program—General

The Future of Social Security, 2/99, (05-10055)
Schedule of Social Security Benefit Payments 1999 & 2000, 1/99, (05-10031)
Social Security Update 1999, 1/99, (05-10003)
Social Security: 24-Hour Telephone Service, 3/99, (05-10082)

Social Security: How You Earn Credits, 1/99, (05-10072)
Social Security: Basic Facts, 3/98, (05-10080)
Social Security: An Employer's Investment, 1/97, (05-10059)
Social Security: Facts and Figures, 4/98, (05-10011)
Social Security: Getting in Touch, 12/97, (05-10048)
Social Security: How It's Financed, 5/98, (05-10094)
Social Security: Report to Our Customers, 9/96, (05-10617)
Social Security: A "Snapshot," 3/98, (05-10006)
Social Security: Understanding the Benefits, 1/99, (05-10024)
Social Security: What Every Woman Should Know, 9/98, (05-10127)
Social Security: When You'll Get Your Benefit, 5/97, (05-10031)
Social Security: Your Taxes . . . What They Are Paying for and Where the Money Goes, 1/99, (05-10010)

The Appeals Process

Appeals, 4/99, (05-10041)
How to File an Unfair Treatment Complaint, 5/93, (05-10017)
Your Right to Representation, 3/98, (05-10075)

Disability Benefits

Disability, 5/96, (05-10029)
Disability Based on Drug Addiction or Alcoholism, 5/96, (05-10047)
A Guide to Social Security and SSI Disability Benefits for People with HIV Infection, 5/97, (05-10020)
How Social Security Can Help with Vocational Rehabilitation, 6/7, (05-10050)
How We Decide If You Are Still Disabled, 4/96, (05-10053)
How Worker's Compensation and Other Disability Payments May Affect Your Benefits, 6/97, (05-10018)
Project ABLE: Able Beneficiaries' Link to Employers, 12/97, (05-10056)
Reviewing Your Disability, 6/97, (05-10068)
Social Security: Benefits for Children with Disabilities, 4/96, (05-10026)
Social Security: If You are Blind How We Can Help, 6/96, (05-10052)
Social Security: What You Need to Know When You Get Disability Benefits, 6/98, (05-10153)
Social Security Benefits for People Living with HIV/AIDS, 5/95, (05-10019)
Social Security Disability Programs Can Help, 9/95, (05-10057)
Receive Your Benefits by Direct Deposit, 1/99, (05-10123)
Working While Disabled . . . How We Can Help, 2/98, (05-10095)

Retirement Benefits

Retirement Benefits, 2/99, (05-10035)
Government Pension Offset, 1/99, (05-10007)
How Work Affects Your Benefits, 1/92, (05-10069)
How Your Retirement Benefit is Figured, 3/99, (05-10070)

Medicare, 6/96, (05-10043)
A Pension from Work Not Covered by Social Security, 1/99, (05-10045)
Receiving Your Benefits by Direct Deposit, 1/99, (05-10123)
Social Security: What You Need to Know When You Get Retirement or Survivors Benefits, 1/99, (05-10077)
Special Payments After Retirement, 3/99, (05-10063)

Social Security Number

Changing Your Name?, 4/95, (05-10642)
Lawfully Admitted Aliens—When You Need a Social Security Number and When You Don't, 4/97, (05-10096)
Social Security: Numbers for Newborns, 7/96, (01-10023)
Social Security: Your Number, 2/98, (05-10002)
When Someone Misuses Your Social Security Number, 3/98, (05-10064)

Supplemental Security Income Program (SSI)

A Desktop Guide to SSI Eligibility Requirements, 1/99, (05-11001)
Food Stamps and Other Nutrition Programs, 3/98, (05-10100)
Food Stamp Facts, 3/98, (05-10101)
A Guide to Social Security and SSI Disability Benefits for People with HIV Infection, 5/97, (05-10020)
How Worker's Compensation and Other Disability Payments May Affect Your Benefits, 6/97, (05-10018)
The Definition of Disability for Children, 7/97, (05-11053)
Receiving Your Benefits by Direct Deposit, 1/77, (05-10123)
Reviewing Your Disability, 6/97, (05-10068)
Social Security: What You Need to Know When You Get SSI, 1/99, (05-11011)
Social Security: Working While Disabled . . . A Guide to Plans for Achieving Self-Support, 1/97, (05-11017)
Social Security: You May Be Able to Get SSI, 1/99, (05-11069)
Supplemental Security Income, 1/97, (05-11000)
Supplemental Security Income for Non-Citizens, 11/97, (05-11051)

Survivors Benefits

Government Pension Offset, 1/99, (05-10007)
Social Security: What You Need to Know When You Get Retirement or Survivors Benefits, 1/99, (05-10077)
Survivors, 10/96, (05-10084)

Bibliography

Alexander, Eben, Jr., M.D. "The 'Retired' Chairman Syndrome: A Twentieth Century Disease." *The Pharos* (summer 1984): 16–19.

Autry, James A. *The Spirit of Retirement.* Roseville, Calif.: Prima Publishing, 2002.

Beck, S. H. "Adjustment To and Satisfaction with Retirement." *Journal of Gerontology* 37 (1982): 137–39.

Beehr, T. A. "The Process of Retirement: A Review and Recommendations for Future Investigation." *Personnel Psychology* 39 (1986): 46–48.

Begley, Sharon, with Erica Check. "Rewiring Your Gray Matter." *Newsweek,* 1 January 2000, 63–65.

Benitez-Silva, Hugo. *Job Search Behavior at the End of the Life Cycle.* State University of New York at Stony Brook: August 2002.

Bridges, William. *Transitions.* Reading, Pa.: Addison-Wesley, 1980.

Buote, Brenda. "Punching the Clock, Part Two." *Boston Globe*, 1 August 2002, N2–N3.

Callenbach, Ernest, and Christine Leefeldt. *The Art of Friendship.* New York: Pantheon Books, 1979.

Dawis, R. V., and L. H. Lofquist. *A Psychological Theory of Work Adjustment: Individual Differences Model and its Applications.* Minneapolis: University of Minnesota Press, 1984.

Durrell, Lawrence. *Bitter Lemons.* New York: Dutton, 1957.

Erikson, Erik. *Identity, Youth and Crisis.* New York: Norton, 1968.

Everyday Psychologist. *The Psychology of Retirement: How to Cope Successfully with a Major Life Transition.* Arlington Heights, Ill.: Business Psychology Research Institute Press, 1999.

Floyd, F. J., S. N. Doll, D. Winemiller, C. Lemsky, T. M. Burgy, M. Werle, and

N. Heilman. "Assessing Retirement Satisfaction and Perceptions of Retirement Experiences." *Psychology and Aging* 7 (1992): 141–43.

Fouquereau, E., A. Fernandez, and E. Mulet. "The Retirement Satisfaction Inventory: Factor Structure in a French Sample." *European Journal of Psychological Assessment* 15, no. 1 (1999): 176–78.

Freedman, Marc. *Prime Time: How Baby Boomers Will Revolutionize Retirement and Transform America.* Washington, D.C.: Public Affairs, 2000.

Haider, Steven, and David Loughrin. *Elderly Labor Supply: Work or Play?* Boston: Boston College, Center for Retirement Research, WP Series No. 2001–04, September 2001.

Harris, Maria. *Jubilee Time.* New York: Bantam Books, 1995.

Heilbrun, Carolyn G. *The Last Gift of Time: Life Beyond Sixty.* New York: Ballantine Books, 1998.

Jackson, Tom. *The Perfect Resume.* New York: Doubleday, 1981.

Johnson, Richard P. *Creating a Successful Retirement.* Liguori, Mo.: Liguori Publications, 1999.

———.*The Twelve Keys to Spiritual Vitality: Powerful Lessons in Living Agelessly.* Liguori, Mo.: Liguori Publications, 1998.

Johnson, R. T., and H. C. Riker. "Retirement Maturity: A Valuable Concept for Pre-retirement Counselors." *Personnel and Guidance Journal* (January 1981): 62–66.

Jones, J. W. *High-Level Positive Retirement: An Education Program for Pre-retirement Planning.* Arlington Heights, Ill.: BPRI Press, 1998.

Kim, S., and D. C. Feldman. "Healthy, Wealthy, or Wise: Predicting Actual Acceptance of Early Retirement Incentives at Three Points in Time." *Personnel Psychology* 51, no. 3 (1998): 43–48.

Klaus, Carl H. *Taking Retirement: A Beginner's Diary.* Boston: Beacon Press, 1999.

Kuczynski, Alex. "They Conquered, They Left." *New York Times,* 24 March 2002, 1, 7.

Maddi, S., and S. Kobasa. *The Hardy Executive: Health Under Stress.* Homewood, Ill.: Dow-Jones Irwin, 1984.

Menduno, M. "Retirement Plans Go Online." *The Industry Standard,* 2–9 August 1999, 2–3.

Moen, Phyllis. "Americans Retiring Earlier But Living Longer." *Successful Aging.* Cornell News Service, February 1996.

Mutran, E. J., D. C. Reitzes, and M. E. Fernandez. "Factors That Influence Attitudes toward Retirement." *Research on Aging* 19 (1997): 3.

Newman, Betsy Kyte. *Getting Unstuck: Moving Ahead With Your Career.* Needham Heights, Mass.: Pearson Custom Publishing, 2000.

———. *Now That You're All Grown Up, What Do You Want To Be?* Dubuque, Iowa: Kendall/Hunt Publishing Company, 1996.

Parker, Yana. *Damn Good Resume Guide: A Crash Course in Resume Writing.* Berkeley, Calif.: Ten Speed Press, 1996.

Pogrebin, Letty Cottin. *Getting over Getting Older: An Intimate Journey.* New York: Little, Brown and Co., 1996.

Putnam, Robert. *Bowling Alone: The Collapse and Revival of American Community.* New York: Simon and Schuster, 2000.

Redd, Robert O. *Achievers Never Quit: How to Create a Life Plan for the Years After Fifty.* Ada, Mich.: Thornapple Publishing Co., 1989.

Rich, Phil, Dorothy Sampson, and Dale Fetherling. *The Healing Journey through Retirement.* New York: John Wiley & Sons, 2000.

Russo, Francine. "*Buddy System.*" *Time* Magazine, 20 January 2002, G1–G3.

Savishinsky, Joel S. *Breaking the Watch: The Meanings of Retirement in America.* Ithaca, N.Y.: Cornell University Press, 2000.

Selye, H. *Stress Without Distress.* Philadelphia: Lippincott, 1974.

Shagrin, Steven, ed. *Facts about Retiring in the United States.* New York: H. W. Wilson, 2001.

Taylor, Carter, and K. Cook. "Adaptation to Retirement: Role Changes and Psychological Resources." *The Career Development Quarterly* 44 (1995): 63–66.

Trollope, Anthony. *The Fixed Period.* Reprint. Ann Arbor, Mich.: University of Michigan Press, 1990.

Tyre, Peg. "R Is for Retirement." *Newsweek*, 10 June 2002, 48.

Von Haller Gilmer, B. "Planning For Retirement: A Guide for Managers." *Technical Report.* Blacksburg, Va.: Virginia Polytechnic Institute, 1981, 73–75.

Warner, Ralph. *Get A Life: You Don't Need A Million to Retire Well.* Berkeley, Calif.: Nolo Books, 2000.

Weltner, Linda. "Fantasy Energizes Daily Life." Lecture given at Harvard Divinity School, 22 March 2001. Reprinted by Roundtable Press, Wellesley, Mass., 2001.

Whitehead, Evelyn Eaton, and James D. Whitehead. *Christian Life Patterns: The Psychological Challenges and Religious Invitations of Adult Life.* Garden City, N.Y.: Doubleday & Co., 1979.

INDEX

About the Author

BETSY KYTE NEWMAN a consultant in management education and career development, is the Director of Counseling and Career Services in Cincinnati, Ohio. She specializes in career planning, mid-career change, and life transitions.